THE
STYLELIFE
CHALLENGE

THE
STYLELIFE
CHALLENGE

MASTER THE GAME IN 30 DAYS

Neil Strauss

HARPER

NEW YORK • LONDON • TORONTO • SYDNEY

HARPER

HarperCollins books may be purchased for educational, business, or sales promotional use. For information please write: Special Markets Department, HarperCollins Publishers, 10 East 53rd Street, New York, NY 10022.

The information in this book has been carefully researched, and all efforts have been made to ensure accuracy. The authors and the publisher assume no responsibility for any injuries suffered or damages or losses incurred during or as a result of following this information. All information should be carefully studied and clearly understood before taking any action based on the information or advice in this book. You assume full responsibility for the consequences of your own actions. If you can't agree to these terms, do not turn the page.

FIRST EDITION

Designed by Jaime Putorti

Library of Congress Cataloging-in-Publication Data is available upon request.

ISBN: 978-0-06-154043-1
ISBN-10: 0-06-154043-9

07   08   09   10   11   DIX/IM   10   9   8   7   6   5   4   3   2   1

To your mother and father. Feel free to blame them for everything that's wrong with you, but don't forget to give them credit for everything that's right.

CAUTION: DO NOT READ

· ·

THE TEMPTATION TO READ THIS BOOK COVER TO COVER
IN A FEW SITTINGS MAY BE STRONG.

THAT'S NORMALLY HOW BOOKS WORK.

NOT THIS ONE.

FOLLOW THE INSTRUCTIONS ONE DAY AT A TIME.
STUDY THE ATTACHED BRIEFINGS.
PERFORM THE FIELD MISSIONS.

AND DO NOT SKIP AHEAD.

MISSING A SINGLE LESSON OR EXPERIENCE WILL AFFECT
YOUR RESULTS, YOUR GAME, YOUR LIFE.

YOU'VE BEEN WARNED.

....

"All I have to say about the Challenge is, 'Wow.' Before this month, I had never approached a woman or been on a date. I just had three dates in three days, and I have more numbers to follow up on."

—CHALLENGER NAME: DIABOLICAL

"This Challenge has been the most inspirational month in my entire life. I feel like I've achieved so much! Taking into account that all of this happened in just thirty days makes it unbelievable!!! Seriously, this was the only area in my life that kept me from being absolutely at peace or absolutely happy: women!"

—CHALLENGER NAME: TONY23

"Since the Challenge, I've heard I am a winner, amazing, perfect, one of a kind, her soul mate, and unbelievable! Thanks, Neil, for the Challenge!"

—CHALLENGER NAME: GODROCK73

"This is one of the best things I have ever participated in . . . It has been life-changing."

—CHALLENGER NAME: MAIDENMAN

"I've gotten more great responses from girls this week than I've ever had in my whole life. People I know are already telling me I'm different and charismatic now."

—CHALLENGER NAME: SAMX

"I already have a girlfriend, and I have no problems with girls. So why did I do the Challenge? Self-improvement. I must say, it has been an incredible boost, both to my self-confidence and to how others see me. I work as a waiter, and now customers are asking for me, girls are constantly approaching me, my tips are much bigger, and people want me to join their parties all the time. Everyone wants to be with me and in my inner circle, and everyone notices how good I feel about myself—and it wasn't like this before."

—CHALLENGER NAME: RACEHORSE

"She was French-kissing me and asking if she could see me when she gets back on Tuesday. I can't wait. She's not only beautiful but smart and kind. Were it not for Neil and the Stylelife Challenge, this never would have happened."

—CHALLENGER NAME: APOLLO

"Neil Strauss has given me a gift of life. I can't describe anything better. Just thanks."

—CHALLENGER NAME: LIZARD

"Waking up each morning is a treat since I started the Challenge. I have a certain excitement about me, like a child on Christmas morning getting ready to open presents, as I march upstairs to my office to see what's next for today. It's really an experience I'll never forget."

—CHALLENGER NAME: REIGN STORM

"This has been one of the most incredible experiences I have had in my entire life. Thank you so much for literally changing my whole life."

—CHALLENGER NAME: BOY

"This is one of the most rewarding experiences of my life! I am so far out of my comfort zone, words can't describe it! And I'm having more and more fun!"

—CHALLENGER NAME: GRINDER73

"I have done a lot of what I would consider to be intense things in my life, but in a way, this beats just about anything I've done, because it is literally changing my own perception of reality and what is in the realm of possibility for me. I would like to live the Stylelife Challenge every month."

—CHALLENGER NAME: LPIE

"Thank you, Neil . . . You'll be remembered for this forever. This is not just another book or a seminar. This is a really big deal!! One day I'll shake your hand and find a way to really thank you for changing my life!"

—CHALLENGER NAME: GRAND

"Neil, thanks a lot for this life-changing experience . . . Your efforts have had a great impact on my life. Not only will I use the information that I learned in my love life but also in all other aspects of my life."

—CHALLENGER NAME: BYRON

"To be honest, I never thought Neil was going to pull this off. I mean, successfully breaking down the seduction game in thirty steps isn't exactly the easiest thing to do. But Neil did an awesome job. Great material. Great people. Great results."

—CHALLENGER NAME: VELOS

"I have read plenty of dating books and seduction manuals. I think the material presented in the Stylelife Challenge is simply the best of the lot. Kudos to Neil for offering the best."

—CHALLENGER NAME: ALBINO

"I have to say, if you are serious about getting the dating aspect of your life handled, and you consciously don't do, or even read, Neil's Stylelife Challenge, then you need to really look at yourself and ask yourself what it is you truly want. Neil is giving us what no one in history has given."

—CHALLENGER NAME: BIG SEND

CONT

ENTS

INTRODUCTION

Why Are We Here?

I didn't want to write this book.

In fact, it's something I thought I'd never do.

I am as embarrassed to write this as you may be to pick it up. And that's fine. It means we're in this together.

Let me tell you why I'm embarrassed. Then I'll tell you why you're embarrassed. And then we'll agree to move on and recognize that we're here on the same page for a reason.

I spent my teens and most of my twenties lonely, desperate, and woefully inexperienced, sitting mutely on the sidelines while women obsessed over guys whose appeal boggled me.

At the lowest point in my dating career, after a two year dry spell, I actually started surfing mail-order bride catalogs on the internet—Russian, Latin, Asian—bookmarking the pages of girls I thought I could learn to live with. I believed there was nowhere else to turn.

But then I had a reality-shattering experience—one of those moments that altered the course of my life. I discovered a secret society on the internet where men reputed to be the best pickup artists alive met to share tips, tales, and tactics learned in clubs, streets, and bedrooms around the world.

Emboldened by desperation, I disguised my identity, knocked on the door of that world, and it slowly opened. Inside, I dropped prostrate before the masters. I thought they would have the keys to release me from the prison of my own frustrations, fears, and insecurities.

They didn't have those keys. But I wouldn't trade the journey I took for anything. Because it taught me something I never would have realized on my own: that I actually had the keys the whole time. I just didn't know where to find them or how to use them.

When I wrote my account of those years, *The Game*, I thought it was my last word on the subject. I wanted to walk away gracefully. Even though I inadvertently became the top-ranked expert in the pickup community, I prefer to be a student of life, not a professor. I write not to teach but because I enjoy storytelling.

However, this book is not a story, at least not in the proper sense of the word. It is a how-to book. The story is not mine to write, but yours to live. The pages are turned not by plot, but by your own motivation.

The fitness and health industries offer thousands of programs designed to help you reach your physical goals. And there is an enormous and well-established self-help industry for women. The pages of *Cosmopolitan*, the characters on *Sex and the City*, and countless books, talk shows, and businesses exist almost solely to help cope with the challenges that come with being a woman in this world.

The landscape for men, however, is very different. Male sexuality is catered to everywhere in society—from the pages of *Maxim* to billboards selling the good life to the $97 billion porn industry. Everywhere they turn, men are shown images of women they are supposed to desire. Yet there is little advice of substance available to help them learn to attract these women, to figure out who they are, to help them improve their lifestyle and social skills. And considering that our social skills determine the course of our lives—our careers, our friends, our family, our children, our happiness—that's a big area to neglect.

So, even though I had no such intentions when I wrote *The Game,* I started doing a few things in my spare time to help the many guys who reached out to me after its publication, with emails, calls, and letters full of heart-wrenching stories. I coached frustrated teenagers, thirty-year-old virgins, recently divorced businessmen, even rock stars and billionaires. However, the more people I helped, the faster my inbox filled with requests from every corner of the world. Hundreds turned to thousands turned to tens of thousands turned to hundreds of thousands. And most of these guys were not assholes and creeps, but nice guys—the ones women always say they're looking for yet at the same time never seem attracted to.

So I decided to bite the bullet. You're now holding that bullet in your hands.

The Stylelife Challenge is a simple, easy-to-follow guide to approaching and attracting women of quality. Though it is designed for the hardest cases, it has also been proven to work for men who are already successful with women.

There is no method, system, or philosophy behind the Challenge. It is simply what works best and fastest. I have now spent five years gathering this knowledge, living it, and sharing it. I've tested the specific material in this book on over thirteen thousand men of varying ages, nationalities, and backgrounds.

The result: a monthlong workout program for your social, attraction, dating, and seduction skills.

I call it the Stylelife Challenge because it is my challenge to you: *Learn the game in thirty days.*

And I'm hesitant to do this, because just that last sentence alone sounds like I'm turning into one of those guys you see grinning from the covers of self-improvement books.

But if it helps you, then it's worth it. And in thirty days, we can both get on with the rest of our lives.

Now let's move on to your story.

HOW TO PLAY
THE GAME

Throw out everything you know about dating.

If you're reading this book, it's because something in your life hasn't been working. And if something isn't working, there's only one way to fix it for good: Take it completely apart and rebuild it piece by piece. Only then can you make sure that every single component is functioning at its highest level, free of error, with the most up-to-date technology.

So if you're too intimidated to approach women you're attracted to, if you're a virgin, if you've never had a real girlfriend, if you're terminally shy, if you're recovering from a rough breakup or divorce, if you're suffering from a long dry spell, if you're tired of watching other guys have all the fun, if you want to attract higher-quality women, or if you're good with women but still not good enough, welcome to the Stylelife Challenge.

My challenge to you is simple: *Get a date in thirty days.*

Along the way, whatever your experience level may be, you'll receive the skills, tools, confidence, and knowledge to meet and attract almost any woman, any time you want.

I want you to master this part of your life. And to make sure you do, I'm going to hold your hand and walk you through every step along the way.

Why am I doing this? Because after reverse engineering my transformation from lonely to oversexed to just-right, as described in *The Game*, I developed a shortcut that compresses years of learning into a month. It has worked not just for me but for thousands of men—transforming their success with women as well as their success in a much bigger game: life.

Overview

- **The objective:** Get a date in thirty days or less.
- **Who can play:** Anyone seeking more success with women.
- **The cost:** The price of this book—and the willingness to try on some new behaviors and see if they fit.
- **The prize:** The company of quality women, the envy of your peers, the lifestyle you deserve.
- **How to play:** This book contains thirty days of exercises. Set aside at least an hour a day—the days don't actually need to be consecutive—to perform the suggested missions and read the supplementary material.

Guidelines

Your instructions are simple: Every morning, as soon as you wake up, read your missions for the day. They may be primers to study, questions to answer, self-improvement exercises to perform, or field exercises to get you out of the house and approaching women. They begin at a very basic level and grow more advanced as the Stylelife Challenge continues. Think of it as a fitness program for your social life.

If you want to get the most from the Challenge—so that your friends and family will instantly notice the new you—it's important that you complete all of the missions in the order they are presented. Do not read ahead. Some exercises may seem basic; others may seem out of character for you. But each new exercise builds upon the last, so stick with it.

Several missions will require you to read certain guides and articles. These can be found in the supplementary briefing immediately following the breakdown of the day's tasks. Make sure that you read each briefing before proceeding to any corresponding field assignments.

The only other material you need will be a pen and paper—although access to a mirror, a computer with an internet connection, and some way to record your voice will be useful for a few assignments. You may also want to keep a journal.

You will not need any money to compete, but you will need a little time each day to do a few small things that can change your life in the long run. None of these assignments requires much more than an hour, so even if you're working three jobs, you should still be able to do them all. In a pinch, you can always save time by cutting back on all that energy wasted desiring women from afar (in men's magazines, on TV shows, in the street, on the internet) and instead learning what it takes to have them in your life.

Though the Challenge is designed to be completed alone, if you're the type of person who's motivated by communicating with others on the same path, optional discussion boards are available at www.stylelife.com/challenge. You can post all questions, adventures, sticking points, and successes there. My trained coaches, your fellow Challengers, and I will be there to help you. In addition, you'll find video and audio examples demonstrating some of these exercises and approaches. Note that all the additional tools provided to supplement this book are free.

How to Win the Game

You win when, at any point between Day 1 and Day 30, you get a date.

A date is defined as a planned second encounter with a woman you have just met.

For example, if you approach a woman at a bar, exchange phone numbers, and meet her for coffee two days later, that is a date.

If you talk to a woman at the mall and arrange to meet that night at a bar, and she shows up specifically to see you, that is a date. Even if you don't exchange phone numbers.

Basically, any scenario where you approach a woman and she agrees to see you at a later date or time—and shows up—constitutes a date.

Once you get a date, feel free to put your name in the winner's circle at www.stylelife.com/challenge and share your story. If you win before the thirty days are up, feel free to continue the Challenge and carry out the daily missions for the remainder of the month. They'll only further enhance your confidence and game.

When you're ready to receive your first mission, turn the page and begin the Stylelife Challenge.

Enjoy, and play fair.

THE
STYLELIFE
CHALLENGE

. . . .

DAILY MISSIONS

DAY

1

MISSION 1: Evaluate Yourself

Fitness programs require you to weigh in on the first day. Financial plans ask for a list of your assets and debts. So to revamp your social life, you'll need to make a social assessment of yourself.

Your first mission is to write answers to the following questions. Don't worry about what anyone else will think of your answers. Your goal is to be as honest with yourself as possible.

1. Write one or two sentences describing how you believe other people currently perceive you.

   _____

   _____

   _____

2. Write one or two sentences describing how you'd like to be perceived by others.

   _____

   _____

   _____

3. List three of your behaviors or characteristics you would like to change.

   _____

   _____

   _____

4. List three new behaviors or characteristics you would like to adopt.

_____

_____

_____

_____

MISSION 2: Read and Destroy

Before moving on to your first field assignment, it's necessary to eliminate any self-sabotaging beliefs that you may have about interacting with women. Your next task is to read the manifesto titled "The Chains That Bind," included at the end of today's assignments in the Day 1 Briefing.

MISSION 3: Operation Small Talk

Your first field assignment: Make small talk with five strangers today.

It doesn't matter whether they're male or female, young or old, friendly or unfriendly. The stranger can be a businessman in the street, an old lady in the supermarket line, a hostess at a restaurant, or a homeless person.

The goal is simply to start a conversation, with no intent other than filling in the silence with a question or pleasantry. The conversation doesn't have to progress beyond a comment and a response.

If idle chatter doesn't come naturally to you, scan news headlines before you leave the house. Small-talk topics include:

- Weather: "It's beautiful out today. Too bad we're stuck inside."
- Sports: "Did you catch the _____ game last night? I couldn't believe it."
- Current events: "Did you hear that _____? What are they going to think of next?"
- Entertainment: "Have you seen the new _____ movie yet? I wonder if it's any good."

Remember: The answer doesn't matter. Whether you receive a long story or a cursory grunt in response, you've completed the mission simply by opening your mouth and speaking to a stranger.

DAY 1 BRIEFING
THE CHAINS THAT BIND

When it came to meeting women, my biggest enemy was me.

I used to look at myself—five foot six, scrawny, bald, and big nosed—and think there was no way I could compete with all the tall, good-looking guys out there. I was so unhappy that I considered plastic surgery.

But once I started approaching women in streets, bars, clubs, and cafés, I discovered that looks don't matter nearly as much as I'd thought. As long as I was well groomed, all I needed in order to attract just about anyone I wanted was the right personality.

Although it's a dubious achievement to be named in the media as the best pickup artist in the world, one thing it taught me was that I didn't need to change the way I looked. I was doing just fine. In fact, I usually had it easier than big, muscular, square-jawed male models because I was much less threatening and intimidating. I could come in under the radar. In the end, then, my problem wasn't my looks, but my limiting beliefs about my looks.

A limiting belief is something that you believe about yourself, other people, or the world—and although it isn't actually true, the fact that you *think* it is holds you back from experience and success. Any time you tell yourself you "can't" do something that's within the realm of human possibility—that's a limiting belief.

Dispelling limiting beliefs is very easy: Just ask yourself, "Was there ever a time when . . ." and insert your limiting belief. For example, if you believe that you get uncomfortable around beautiful women, ask yourself, "Was there ever a time when I was comfortable around a beautiful woman?" Name just one time, and you've disproved your limiting belief.

Nearly everyone is held back by some limiting belief, whether he's conscious of it or not. So before I send you running around the streets talking to strangers, let's clear the air and dispel a few of the most common limiting beliefs about dating.

LIMITING BELIEF: If I talk to her, she'll ignore me—or, even worse, say something mean that will embarrass me.

REALITY: Here's something that may surprise you: The harder it is for you to approach women, the less likely it is that you'll be rudely rejected.

Why is that? Because most people have been raised to be courteous and polite, unless they feel threatened—and a shy guy isn't too likely to intimidate anyone. The worst thing that's likely to happen is the woman will politely say she's having a private conversation, or simply excuse herself to go to the bathroom. Playing negative what-if scenarios in your head is detrimental to your emotional health. Instead, get out of the house and start approaching women, and you'll discover that most of the things you imagine going wrong will never happen.

LIMITING BELIEF: People are looking at me, judging me, or making fun of me.

REALITY: This is half right. People may notice you, but they're not necessarily judging you—most of them are too busy worrying about what other people are thinking of them. Once you realize that most people are just like you—and that they're actually seeking your approval—you'll start to become socially fearless.

Besides, most bystanders who see you approach a girl or a group assume that you know the people. So act like you do. Not only will it ease your worries about what everyone else is thinking, but it'll also make your approach more effective.

LIMITING BELIEF: Women aren't attracted to nice guys. They like jerks.

REALITY: This is one of the oldest myths about dating. And, fortunately, it's inaccurate. The dating dichotomy isn't actually between nice guys and mean guys, or good boys and bad boys. It's between weak guys and strong guys. Women are drawn to men who demonstrate strength—not necessarily physical strength, but the ability to make them feel safe. So if you're a nice guy, you can still be nice. But you must also be strong.

However, make sure you know what nice means. Most guys who define themselves as "too nice" only behave nicely because they want everybody to like them and don't want anyone to think badly of them. So, if this is you, get off your nice high horse. Don't mistake being fearful and weak-minded for being nice.

LIMITING BELIEF: I'm not good-looking, rich, or famous enough to be with a beautiful woman.

REALITY: There are plenty of rock stars and multimillionaires who have the exact same problems with women that you do. I know because I've coached many of them. And, in the process, I learned that money, looks, and fame—while they certainly make things much easier—aren't actually necessary. Fortunately for men, the way we look doesn't matter nearly as much as how we present ourselves. And this requires only good grooming, and clothing that conveys an attractive identity. When it comes to wealth and fame, simply displaying the desire and ability to achieve them can be just as powerful. Like talent scouts, many women are attracted to men with goals and potential. And in the next ten days, we'll be sharpening your appearance, goals, and perceived potential.

LIMITING BELIEF: There's this one girl . . .
REALITY: There are many incredible women in this world. If you're hung up on one particular girl you just can't get out of your mind—and she hasn't given you any sense that she shares the feelings—then recognize that's not love you're feeling, but obsession. And that obsession is likely to scare her away. The best thing you can do for yourself and for her is to go out and interact with as many women as possible, until you realize that there are plenty of people out there for you—some of whom are capable of recognizing your worth and reciprocating your feelings.

LIMITING BELIEF: Some guys are born with the ability to charm women. Other guys just don't have it and never will.
REALITY: Fortunately, there is a third type of guy: one who can learn it. That's me. And once you understand how attraction works and have a few successful approaches under your belt, it'll be you too. Any problems you may currently be having aren't the result of who you are but of what you're doing and how you're presenting yourself. Those problems can be fixed easily with the right knowledge and a little practice. If you stick with the program after the Challenge, you'll even start doing better than the so-called naturals you once envied.

LIMITING BELIEF: All I have to do is "be myself," and eventually I'll meet the right woman who likes me for me.
REALITY: This works only if you know exactly who you are, what your strengths are, and how to convey them successfully. Most often, this statement is used as an excuse not to improve. What most of us present to the world isn't

necessarily our true self: It's a combination of years of bad habits and fear-based behavior. Our real self lies buried underneath all the insecurities and inhibitions. So rather than just being yourself, focus on discovering and permanently bringing to the surface your best self.

LIMITING BELIEF: To figure out what women want, just ask them.

REALITY: This may be true sometimes, but not as often as many people think. It wasn't until I started trying behaviors that seemed counterintuitive that I discovered a key principle of the game: What women want isn't necessarily what they respond to. Furthermore, what women *say* they want may be what they want in a relationship, but it isn't always what attracts them during the courtship period. That said, most women will give you the information you need to attract them, but it's usually found between the lines.

LIMITING BELIEF: If I approach a woman, she'll know I'm hitting on her and think I'm lame.

REALITY: This is only partially true—women think this only when men approach them *badly*. This includes men who make them uncomfortable, creep them out, or seem to have an agenda. The biggest mistake a man can make with a woman is hitting on her before she's attracted to him. And though this describes the so-called technique of most men, it's a mistake you'll avoid if you follow your daily missions. Few women will resent meeting someone who is warm, funny, sincere, interesting, engaging, makes them feel comfortable, and isn't going to stick around talking their ear off.

LIMITING BELIEF: Women don't like sex as much as men do. They're mostly interested in having a relationship.

REALITY: If you believe that, you haven't spent enough time around women. Here are a few facts that may help dispel that belief: It's women, rarely men, who have an organ solely made for sexual pleasure: the clitoris, which has twice as many nerve endings as a man's entire penis. And it's women, not men, whose orgasms can last minutes or longer. Most men have just one orgasm and then lose their arousal; most women can have orgasm after orgasm and many different types: clitoral, vaginal, blended, full-body, and psycholagnic (look it up).

In short, good sex is even better for women than it is for us. So doesn't it make sense that they want it more?

DAY

2

MISSION 1: Set Your Goals

Congratulations! You survived Day 1.

Whether you already know your life goals or you just need a little prodding, today's first exercise will help you set your intent and program your mind for success.

To quote J. C. Penney, founder of the department store chain, "Give me a stock clerk with a goal, and I'll give you a man who will make history. Give me a man with no goals, and I'll give you a stock clerk."

Your mission is to read the following questions, think about them carefully, and write your personal mission statement. Be as specific and ambitious as possible. (Examples of accomplishments include starting a band, buying a house, getting in shape, launching a business, becoming president.)

1. What three accomplishments would you like to achieve to make you happier?

   _____

   _____

   _____

   _____

2. What are the reasons these accomplishments will make you happier?

   _____

   _____

   _____

   _____

3. What is your personal mission?

I will become _____ (maximum four words)
　　　　　　　　MY ROLE

who will _____ (maximum four words)
　　　　MY CLAIM TO FAME

within _____ days/weeks/years.
　　　　NUMBER

4. List three specific results that will let you know that you've accomplished your mission. (For example, "I will have earned $200,000," "I will have lost thirty pounds," or "I will have won five Academy Awards.")

1. I will have _____ _____ _____.
　　　　　　ACTION VERB　　　NUMBER　　ASPECT
2. I will have _____ _____ _____.
　　　　　　ACTION VERB　　　NUMBER　　ASPECT
3. I will have _____ _____ _____.
　　　　　　ACTION VERB　　　NUMBER　　ASPECT

5. Why are you now fully committed to pursuing your personal mission?

Because if I *don't* pursue it *now*, I will continue to suffer over the next years and

■ my _____ will decrease/get worse/fail.
　　ELEMENT/QUALITY OF LIFE

■ my _____ will decrease/get worse/fail.
　　ELEMENT/QUALITY OF LIFE

■ my _____ will decrease/get worse/fail.
　　ELEMENT/QUALITY OF LIFE

But if I *do* pursue it *now*, I will enjoy the next years and

■ my _____ will increase/improve/come true.
　　ELEMENT/QUALITY OF LIFE

■ my _____ will increase/improve/come true.
       ELEMENT/QUALITY OF LIFE

■ my _____ will increase/improve/come true.
       ELEMENT/QUALITY OF LIFE

MISSION 2: Look into Your Eyes (Optional)

There's another step you can take to reinforce your personal mission statement and strengthen your subconscious intent: self-hypnosis. I've commissioned a charismatic mind-shaping exercise specifically for the Challenge, which I've made available for you online at www.stylelife.com/challenge.

After you download it, find a comfortable place free of distraction. Dim the lights, take off your shoes, and sit or lie down. Relax. Then put on headphones, play the audio, and take the journey.

Make sure you listen to the entire recording without interruption. It's more important to *feel* this experience than to see it. Try to listen to the recording every other day during the Challenge: The more you repeat it, the better the result.

MISSION 3: Look into Their Eyes

Your field assignment today is to go out and make small talk with five more strangers.

But, this time, there's one more thing you need to do: make eye contact with each person. Record his or her eye color in the space below:

1. _____
2. _____
3. _____
4. _____
5. _____

In the first small-talk exercise, the purpose was to develop the ability to talk to anyone without fear. Meeting people eye to eye (being careful not to stare) will not only increase the likelihood of a response, it'll help you connect with them on a more personal level.

If you'd like to develop this crucial but subtle skill further, here's an extra-credit exercise: Try to hail a cab, get a bartender's attention, or call a waiter to your table without speaking or gesturing—instead, use nothing but eye contact.

MISSION 4: A Hint for Tomorrow

Be sure to read tomorrow's assignment the moment you wake up—before you shower, shave, or check your email.

DAY 3

MISSION 1: Adopt the Caveman Hygiene Method

This next mission may make you a little uncomfortable. And that's a good thing. The reason will be made clear tomorrow. But for now:

Do not shower today.

Do not shave today.

Chances are, no one will notice—most people are too busy worrying about how they look. If they do, tell them you're trying to win a bet or participating in a highly compensated study for the deodorant industry.

MISSION 2: Speak with Confidence

When I was learning the game, I had trouble meeting new people because I talked too fast, too softly, and swallowed my words. In a loud club, it made meeting women practically impossible. So I went to a vocal coach named Arthur Joseph.

"Your voice is your identity," he teaches. "It can tell people everything about who you are, how you feel about yourself, and what you believe in."

So today we're going to work on your voice.

There are five common speech mistakes people make. These errors are outlined, along with an exercise for each, in your Day 3 Briefing.

Your task is to read the article and do at least three of the exercises, even if you don't think you need to. You may be surprised.

MISSION 3: Find Mr. Moviefone

For today's field mission, stay home. You're going to use only your voice.

Your task is to dial a local number randomly on your telephone. When someone answers, try to get him or her to recommend a good movie. That's all.

The point isn't just to talk to more strangers. It's to learn how to change the course of an interaction without making the other person feel uncomfortable.

This skill will help you take control of conversations in real life and direct them toward the outcome you want.

A few hints:

Rather than just dialing random strings of seven-digit numbers, look through a residential telephone book and select numbers at random. Or use the first three digits in your own number and make up the last four digits.

Here's a sample script I used when doing the Challenge myself:

"Hi, is Katie there? No? Well, maybe I can quickly ask you this instead." Don't pause here and give the person an opportunity to say no. "I want to see a movie tonight. And I was wondering, have you seen any good movies lately that you'd recommend?"

Here's another script that worked.

"Hello? Is this Moviefone? No? Well, would you mind quickly recommending a movie to watch tonight? Have you seen anything good lately?"

If the person you're speaking to hesitates or asks if this is a joke, reassure him or her by saying that you're serious. One magic word you can use is *because*. Providing a reason, no matter how illogical (such as "No, I'm serious, because I'm in a rush"), psychologically influences people to accept an unexpected behavior.

Once you've received a movie recommendation from three separate people, consider today's mission successfully completed.

MISSION 4: Hypno Time (Optional)

Listen to yesterday's charismatic mind-shaping exercise again. Understand and begin to integrate your new attributes and self-image.

DAY 3 BRIEFING
VOCAL TRAINING

With the help of several vocal coaches, I've put together five exercises designed to eliminate weakness in your speech and bring out your most full, powerful, and commanding voice.

Before beginning this activity, you'll need:

- A mirror, preferably full-length;
- An audio recorder, or a computer with a microphone;
- An open area where you can be loud.

The Basics

There are two factors that make all the difference between a good orator and a bad one: breath and posture.

Breathing deeply before you speak fills your lungs with air, allowing you to give full power to your words. To ensure that you're doing this correctly, take a deep breath. If your chest expands, your breathing is too shallow.

Try it again until your diaphragm—the sheet of muscle beneath your rib cage—expands. To check this, place your hand on your stomach to make sure it rises with each inhalation.

Bad posture can restrict your diaphragm and breathing, effectively neutering your vocal power. Whenever you speak, make sure that your upper body is straight and aligned. If necessary, use the technique of imagining a string running from the bottom of your spine to the top of your head and then pulling it taut. But don't get too tense; make sure you're relaxed comfortably into the frame of your body. If this seems unnatural, don't worry: Tomorrow we'll examine your posture in detail.

PROBLEM: Low or Soft Voice
   SOLUTION: Find a large, open space indoors or outdoors. Bring an audio recorder, a trusted friend, or both.

Take three large steps away from your audio recorder or friend.

Take a deep breath from your diaphragm. Hold it, then slowly exhale.

Take two more deep breaths. Then inhale one more time, and as you exhale, say, using your everyday voice, "I can say this without shouting and still be heard."

Now go back and listen to your voice on the recording, or ask your friend how you sounded.

Return to the same position and recite the same line. This time, instead of speaking to your friend or the recorder, aim your voice at a spot six to ten feet above. Imagine your voice is a football, traveling a wide arc to make a field goal. Afterward, check the results for improvement.

Take three more large steps away and repeat the same sentence: "I can say this without shouting and still be heard." Try to increase the volume of your voice without screaming or changing the tone.

Take another three steps away. Remember to send your voice in a high arc, past the listener. Afterward, listen to your recording (or your friend's reaction) and critique your vocal projection. See how far away you can stand and still be heard clearly without shouting. Practice this until you're comfortable talking at loud volumes without changing the tone of your voice. You'll notice that, in the process, you'll begin to speak more clearly as well.

If you've been a quiet talker all your life, chances are that the volume of your voice in your head isn't the volume at which other people hear you. So if you normally talk at a 5, from now on take it up to a 7. Don't worry about speaking too loudly. It's much more likely that your friends will start complimenting you on how clearly you've started communicating.

PROBLEM: Fast Speech

SOLUTION: Speaking too rapidly is one of the most common and crippling vocal mistakes. Not only does it make you difficult to understand, but it gives others the impression that you're nervous, you're not confident, and what you have to say is unimportant.

A calm, slow voice commands authority.

For this exercise, sit up straight in front of your audio recorder or computer microphone. Take a deep breath. Now say without slowing down the following sentence—all in one breath: "I will no longer speak too quickly and cram all my words together in one breath because I have lots of thoughts in my head and I am trying to get them all out and I am afraid that if I pause, people will stop listening."

Listen to the recording. Most likely, cramming a run-on sentence into one breath worsened your enunciation and caused you to swallow some words.

Now inhale and say the same line. But this time, make the pace exaggeratedly slow and deliberate; leave excruciatingly long pauses between phrases; pronounce each word carefully; and take a breath more often than you feel you need to. Then listen to the recording.

Repeat this exercise five to ten times, gradually increasing the pace, normalizing your breathing, and shortening the pauses between words while making sure you're still speaking slowly and pronouncing each word fully. This is going to feel unnatural at first, but stick with it until you find a comfortable and clear speaking pace that captures the attention of others.

Repeat the run-on sentence several more times in front of a mirror until you get used to your new speaking pace.

After you've mastered this exercise on your own, your voice may well speed up again in social situations. So make sure you monitor yourself, and take a breath and slow down as soon as you catch yourself speed talking.

Just like turning up the volume on your voice, it may take a while for your inner ear to get used to this change. You may think you're boring others, but you're not. Fast speakers often discover that, even when they've slowed down to what seems like an interminable crawl, they're still talking faster than everyone else in the room.

PROBLEM: Brain Farts

SOLUTION: Brain farts, or pausers, are the enemy of confidence.

Whether or not you know what a brain fart is, try this exercise before reading any further: Record yourself speaking with a friend. Either take an audio recorder with you when you leave the house, or record your end of the conversation next time you're on the phone.

Play back the recording and carefully transcribe the first few sentences. Make sure you write down every single word you say. Don't leave out anything.

Now take a look at what you've written. Do you notice the words *um* or *uh* anywhere? How about "you know," "like," or "whatever"? These are known as pausers, or brain farts.

We've learned to use these meaningless utterances for several reasons: as placeholders, to make sure we don't lose anyone's attention while we're thinking of what to say next, and as a sonar system, to make sure the other person understands or agrees with what we're saying.

But do you know what message these pausers actually send to others? Insecurity.

Pausing for a moment won't cause you to lose someone's attention. Always speak as if you're making complete sense—even when you don't think you are. The fact is, the way you communicate makes more of an impression than what you say.

Now listen to ten minutes of the conversation you recorded. Write down every pauser you say, then read them out loud (unless the sheet is blank, in which case you should apply for work as a newscaster immediately). Repeat them until they're imprinted in your mind so that you'll be conscious of them during future conversations. From now on, slow down and consciously choose each word when speaking.

The secret to eliminating pausers—and to breaking most other bad habits—is to become self-correcting. In other words, listen to yourself when you speak. If you notice a brain fart, stop, correct yourself, and repeat the sentence without the pauser. It may also help to carry your list of pausers with you, as a reminder to monitor your speech for these small signifiers of insecurity.

PROBLEM: Monotone Voice

SOLUTION: If you drone like an old geography teacher when you speak; if your friends close their eyes when you tell a story; if your colleagues tune out halfway through your presentations, you just may have a monotone voice.

Here's an excerpt from a children's short story. Read it out loud into your audio recorder now:

> *Leopold Elfin had a problem: His nose whistled. He couldn't help it. Every time he breathed through his nose, out came a note. Not the quiet hiss that occasionally issues from the hoary nostrils of men three times his age, but a loud, shrill shriek like a crossing guard blowing for traffic to stop. Leopold was well aware of this problem, but he'd never been to see a doctor, figuring it was more a matter of anatomy than medicine. Maybe it was his*

pinched septum, his narrow oval nostrils, or the crook at the bridge of his nose that was responsible for his one social impropriety.

Now play back the recording. If possible, listen to it with a friend or family member to get a more objective opinion.

Do you have a dynamic storytelling voice, the kind that sucks listeners into the world you're describing? Or do you have a monotone voice, the kind that listeners tend to tune out?

If it's the latter, then turn on the television. Find a male host, comedian, or other broadcaster with a dynamic voice that you like. Listen to him speak. Pay attention to every detail and nuance that make his voice compelling. Notice how he is present in the material, how his voice rings with energy, warmth, and immediacy.

Next, try repeating what he says, using exactly his words, tone, and style.

When you feel you're able to convey a few of his engaging qualities, go back to the story excerpt. Read it again into the recorder, using the techniques you just learned. Experiment with changing the volume, pitch, speed, timbre, rhythm, and flow of your voice as you read. Try emphasizing different words; creating pauses where they don't normally belong; shortening or elongating words; and speaking in different voices and accents. Read the excerpt several times, and don't be afraid to get silly if it helps you break through your limitations.

When you're finished, read the paragraph once more. This time, imagine you're recording a book on tape for children. Compare this new version to your original version—and discover the great storyteller lurking inside you.

PROBLEM: Statements that Sound like Questions

SOLUTION: Sit down, pull out your trusty recorder, and place it in front of you.

For your final vocal exercise, imagine that the audio recorder is your friend. And this friend of yours doesn't like fish. Your goal is to convince him to try sushi with you tonight.

When you're finished, play back the recording. Listen carefully. Does your voice rise in pitch at the end of any declarative sentences?

If it does, you'll notice that your statements sound like questions. And that makes you seem unsure of yourself.

Persuasive speakers end their sentences—and their argument—conclusively.

If your statements end in a higher pitch than they started, record the same speech again. This time, be firm. Instead of asking questions that beg for affirmation, make definitive statements that demonstrate your conviction. And make sure that the speech itself doesn't trail off into extraneous blather and repetition but instead comes to a definite and powerful conclusion. Sound like you know what you're talking about and believe every word you say. Even if you don't happen to like sushi.

When you have this mastered, you're done.

Congratulations.

However, just because you were able to identify and correct these five major vocal mistakes today doesn't mean the problem is solved for good. Revisit these exercises twice a week. And whenever you're in conversation, monitor your posture, breathing, and speech. If you catch yourself backsliding, correct yourself immediately. Before long, you'll not only have women hanging on your every word, you'll have your own radio talk show.

DAY

4

MISSION 1: Hit the Showers

As soon as you wake up, put on your favorite upbeat music and play it loud. Shower, shampoo, and soap thoroughly. Wash twice if you want. And . . . don't masturbate today, if you're prone to doing so.

Put something scented on your body: moisturizer, talcum powder, or a light spritz of cologne. Gargle with mouthwash. Whatever makes you feel and smell good.

Then shave your face clean (preserving any preexisting mustache, beard, or goatee). Make sure you shave or tweeze any stray places where you sprout hair—your ears, nostrils, the back of your neck.

Put on clean, well-fitting clothing. You should feel like a million dollars.

Now look at yourself in the mirror and read the following to yourself:

"You are amazing. People love you and respect you. You radiate charisma, charm, and grace. You stand out from everyone around you. Talking to you is a privilege. And you deserve the best the world has to offer. It's all there out there, waiting for you."

Read it as many times as it takes—say it out loud if you have to—until you truly feel and embody it.

Now hold on to that feeling . . .

MISSION 2: Ask an Expert

What you experienced in the previous mission is a simple ritual that helps many men enter a state of increased confidence, positivity, and unassailability. Take a moment to develop your own ritual to pump yourself up before going out to meet women. It may involve exercising, cleaning, repeating affirmations, reading something inspirational, replaying previous successes in your mind, blasting your favorite music, singing, showering, dancing, calling someone who makes you laugh, or any combination of the above.

This is the first day you're going to meet women you could possibly date. You should make these approaches at the earliest possible opportunity after leaving the house clean, well shaven, and feeling good about yourself.

Your mission: Ask three women to recommend a cool local clothing store that carries menswear. Your mission is complete once you've approached three women *and* received one clothing store recommendation. (In other words, if you approach three women and you get a clothing store suggestion, you're done. If you approach three women and you don't get a clothing store recommendation, keep asking until you do.)

When you get a recommendation, write down the name of the store, and the location if she knows it. Make sure you keep the name and location handy.

Here are a few tips:

- Approach women who seem like they live in town and have a cool sense of style.
- If you're talking to people in the street, don't approach them from behind, which can be startling. Either approach them from the front, or walk ahead of them and turn your head back over your shoulder as you keep walking. They'll feel even more comfortable if you increase the distance as you walk, as if you have somewhere to be. You may also approach in cafés, shopping malls, or wherever you're comfortable.
- Be aware that only about 1 in 3 women will be able to think of a store right away. Some people go blank when put on the spot.

As soon as she answers, even if it's just to say "I don't know," you've made your approach. Tell her "Thanks for your help" (or "Thanks anyway" if she doesn't have any ideas) and leave if you want. Or continue the interaction. The choice is yours.

Good luck.

MISSION 3: Stand Up Straight

Before you even open your mouth, a woman has formed an initial impression of you. And that impression is based largely on your body language. Today you're going to learn to carry yourself with confidence through a simple posture exercise known as the wall stance.

Stand with your back against a wall. Make sure your heels, butt, and shoulders are touching the wall. In addition, the back of your head just above the level of your chin should be against the wall.

Remain in this position for a minute. Reach behind your back and check to make sure there isn't too much space between your lower back and the wall. If there is, tighten your abdomen to bring the small of your back closer to the wall.

Now move away from the wall, and walk around the room for a minute without changing your posture. Commit the position and alignment of your body to memory.

Repeat this exercise one more time today and, if possible, once a day throughout the Challenge. From now on, check your posture on a regular basis, and bring yourself into alignment if you catch yourself slouching.

Because posture is key not just to your confidence and appearance but also to your health, I've prepared an extra-credit video tutorial for you online at www.stylelife.com/challenge. It provides the basics on Alexander Technique, a school of movement that improves not just the way you stand, walk, and sit but also the way you speak and feel about yourself.

DAY

5

MISSION 1: Here Comes the Groom

Today is grooming day, and the focus is your appearance.

When men discuss attraction skills, they often act as if looks are the only variable out of their control, perhaps because they feel that appearance is genetic. Not true.

Just as any girl can slim down, get breast implants, and dye her hair blonde to turn heads, any guy can become good looking. In the same way you can learn openers, routines, and confidence, you can learn looks. No matter how you're perceived right now, if you're willing to make a few changes, you can be considered good looking.

I've taken worst-case scenarios—fat, balding, acne-plagued guys in Coke bottle glasses—and through the miracles of tanning, contacts, head shaving, dermatology, health clubs, and menswear, turned them into cool, good-looking men who exude confidence and power.

Now it's your turn.

Your assignment is to read the grooming checklist in your Day 5 Briefing. Then perform at least one task on the checklist. Not all the suggestions will apply to you, so choose one from the area in which you're most deficient.

If you have a trustworthy female friend, ask her: "If you had to pick one thing to change about the way I groom myself, what would it be?" Let her know you'd sincerely appreciate an honest, constructive answer—and make sure you don't take it personally when she gives you one.

MISSION 2: Make a Change

The first step to better looks is better grooming. The second is committing to the right style.

Ideally, you want your style and clothing to convey that you belong to one of three segments of society: the same niche, group, or tribe that the woman you're interested in belongs to; a tribe she wants to belong to; or a tribe she wants to visit. For example, men in dirty oversized undershirts and ill-fitting khaki shorts belong to few women's tribes, while pierced, tattooed rock stars belong to a tribe that most women at least want to visit.

Thus, your mission today is to get a free style consultation.

Do this by examining the results of yesterday's field exercise and selecting the clothing store that received the highest recommendation. If possible, avoid large chains. Choose a small independent store instead.

Go to the clothing store—preferably when it's least likely to be crowded—and speak to the saleswoman who seems the most helpful. Tell her you want to change your style, and ask her to put together a complete outfit for you. If she wants you to be more specific, tell her you're going to a high-profile fashion show, art opening, movie premiere, trendy club, or whatever imaginary event best suits the new you.

Change into the new outfit and observe yourself in the mirror. Though the style of the clothing matters, a perfect fit is more important.

If you truly detest the clothing, tell her why and ask her to put together another outfit. If the saleswoman isn't helpful or pushes you too hard to buy, go to another store.

If you like the outfit and can afford it, buy it. When you get home, make sure you take care of it by hanging it in a closet and dry-cleaning it when it's dirty.

If the clothes are beyond your means, remember the brands, sizes, and styles, so you can either buy them in the future, find equivalent items at a used-clothing store, or order them cheaper online.

If you choose to buy the outfit, ask the saleswoman where you can find a nice pair of shoes. At the shoe store, show an employee the outfit and ask for sharp shoes that match it.

MISSION 3: Brush Up

Choose one of the following to experience again: the mind-shaping audio, vocal exercises, or posture wall stance and video. Try to review at least one of these fundamentals every day during the Challenge.

MISSION 4: Lay Out Your School Clothes

If you bought any new clothing or accessories today, be prepared to wear them tomorrow.

DAY 5 BRIEFING
GROOMING CHECKLIST

Choose at least one of the items on this list and make the suggested change. Not all of these tips will apply to everyone. Some are overly remedial; others are extremely meticulous. A few of the tips you'll be able to implement in just a few minutes at no cost; others may take time or money. Avoid the tasks you're most comfortable with. It's the changes you're uncomfortable with that will lead to the most improvement.

- **Change your hairstyle.** Look through music and men's fashion magazines, find the haircut you'd most like to have, and make an appointment at the best beauty salon in town. Bring the photo with you. Make sure you ask your hairstylist to recommend any hair product necessary to maintain your new look.
- **Ditch the glasses.** Get contacts or laser surgery. If your glasses complement your style, consider getting cool designer frames.
- **Get tan.** The quickest and easiest way to do this is to get a spray-tan at a tanning salon. Make sure they use a relatively realistic-looking brand, like Mystic Tan.
- **Get a manicure and pedicure.** Go to any nail salon. It isn't necessary to get a colored polish; just ask to get your nails buffed or request a clear top coat. Not only does this convey good grooming, but it will help you understand that the reason a woman pays attention

to the small details on you is that she pays attention to those details on herself.

■ **Remove excess hair.** Get tweezers or a nose-hair trimmer, and remove any hair in your nostrils, between your eyebrows, in your ears, and on the back of your neck. If you're particularly hirsute elsewhere, trim it, shave it, or pluck it.

■ **Examine yourself closely in a mirror.** If possible, buy a magnifying mirror. Remove any visible ear wax with a Q-tip; tweeze any stray hairs; clip and clean your fingernails and toenails; and look for oily skin, dry skin, bags under your eyes, or other problem areas that require the use of specialized facial products.

■ **Manage your eyebrows.** Go to a spa or salon and get your eyebrows tweezed (or waxed), and, optionally, dyed a slightly darker or lighter shade.

■ **Whiten your teeth.** Buy an over-the-counter tooth whitening system, such as Crest Whitestrips, and begin using it tonight. If you haven't seen a dentist in over a year, make an appointment.

■ **Freshen your breath.** Start flossing daily. Consider getting a tongue scraper if halitosis is a problem. Buy gum or mints, and carry them with you at all times.

■ **Get free dermatology advice.** Go to a department store cosmetics counter and ask the beautician what facial products she recommends for your skin type. Feel free to ask for samples or buy cheaper equivalents at a drugstore. If you consider your complexion to be a major liability, make an appointment to see a dermatologist.

■ **Accessorize.** Buy a necklace, rings, a bracelet, a wrist cuff, or any other tasteful accoutrement. Try not to get anything that looks too cheap and mass produced—even if it is. When in doubt, err on the side of wearing something simple for now.

■ **Join a gym.** Make an appointment with a trainer to get a fitness evaluation and exercise regimen that includes both cardiovascular training to reduce fat and resistance training to increase muscle mass. Make working out a borderline obsession.

■ **Eat healthier.** Control your caloric intake and review your diet to limit saturated fats, refined sugars, excess salt, and food high in preservatives and carbohydrates. Eat fresh fruits, vegetables, and lean protein. If you're more than forty percent over the weight you should be, consult a doctor about weight loss options.

- **Make sure your clothes fit.** Go through your closet and try on everything. If jackets drop off your shoulders, jeans droop off your butt, short sleeves stop at your elbows, or shirt necks hang down to your chest, either get the item tailored or donate it to a thrift store. Same goes for anything else that doesn't flatter you. Commit to replacing these items with well-fitting clothes that best suit your build.

If you have any grooming or appearance issue not listed above—be it underarm sweat, foot odor, an unsightly blemish, or your ex-girlfriend's name tattooed on your neck—this is the day to start taking care of it. Research solutions online; talk to fellow Challengers in the Stylelife forum; and, if necessary, pick up recommended products or make that doctor's appointment.

Don't let yourself off the hook when it comes to looks. You no longer have an excuse.

DAY

MISSION 1: Conquering AA

Today we're going to discuss the single most debilitating problem facing would-be Casanovas: approach anxiety.

Approach anxiety is a crippling disease that occurs when a man is confronted by the prospect of approaching an attractive woman. Symptoms include sweaty palms, increased heart rate, shortness of breath, and a lump in the throat. Psychologically speaking, it's less a fear of approaching than a fear of rejection.

If you hesitated before walking up to anyone during any of your field assignments so far, then you have approach anxiety. If you haven't been nervous yet, you probably will as the missions grow more advanced, or when you see that one special girl. It happens to the best of us.

So turn to your Day 6 Briefing while there's still time and read the cure proposed by Don Diego Garcia, a senior coach in the Stylelife Academy.

MISSION 2: If You Can't Say Something Nice . . .

Make sure you shower, shave, and feel good before you leave the house today. If you developed a confidence boosting ritual on Day 4, do it. If you purchased any new items yesterday, put them on. You're going out again.

Your mission: Give four women spontaneous compliments. Two of these women can be people you know—friends, coworkers, even your mother. But two should be strangers.

Avoid general compliments such as "You're beautiful." And avoid saying anything that could be construed as showing sexual interest, like "You're hot." Instead, focus on complimenting something specific, such as her nails, shoes, handbag, or posture. After spending time rigorously examining yourself yesterday, you should find it easier to spot and appreciate these details.

The most common response will be a sincere, polite, or dismissive thank-you. Leave after the compliment, unless she continues the conversation.

The key is to be perceived not as trying to flatter or hit on her but as showing sincere appreciation of something you've noticed spontaneously.

Though giving compliments isn't recommended for all approaches, generating attraction isn't the goal today. This exercise is designed to help eliminate approach anxiety, improve your skills of observation, and get you out of your head and aware of someone else's reality.

MISSION 3: The Eight-hour Rule

Get a good night's sleep, because tomorrow is one of the most crucial days in the Stylelife Challenge.

DAY 6 BRIEFING
ABOLISH APPROACH ANXIETY

By Don Diego Garcia

There are millions of words of wisdom offered by experts on creating and developing a successful intimate relationship, but seven words stand above them all: *You can't win if you don't play.*

That is the bottom line of bottom lines, courtesy of the California State Lottery. If you stay in your solipsistic cave, you will never form a new relationship. You *must* get out of the house and interact with new people.

Approach anxiety is a name for the internal demon that keeps men from talking to attractive strangers when there are no external barriers. Before working on ways to convert approach anxiety into approach excitement, let's discuss two key concepts: the limiting mind and the freedom mind.

The Limiting Mind

When we are born, nature installs two major instinctual fears to keep us safe: a fear of heights and a fear of loud noises.

Fear in moderation is a good thing. It protects us from harm. For example, a fear of heights protects us from falling off cliffs. A fear of loud noises enables us to react quickly to warnings of danger. However, most fears and limits we have are the result not of nature but of nurture. We place limits on ourselves as the result of negative experiences from our childhood and the influence of authority figures.

The Freedom Mind

The biological freedom mind gives us signals of hunger to eat, thirst to drink, and desire to procreate. In modern times, we also have cultural drives for power through career, enjoyment through play, and purpose through spiritual practice.

When our limiting mind and freedom mind are in homeostatic balance, all is good. We live in harmony with the world, effectively solving problems as they arise. But when our freedom mind and limiting mind fall out of balance, all kinds of afflictions arise.

Identify Your Limiting Mind

Most of your limiting mind's beliefs were spoon-fed to you by your parents, guardians, teachers, clergy, peers, or whomever you admired while growing up. While there is some value in tracing the sources of your own personal limiting mind, it's more important to understand its structure. The limiting mind tends to feed on itself in a downward spiral. Placing blame on others or on yourself for the material in your limiting mind only serves to strengthen it. It's best to forgive, forget, and move on.

The first step on most roads to recovery is acceptance—admitting that there's a problem. The second step in overcoming the source of our anxiety is to bring it out of unconscious darkness and into the light of our conscious awareness. Only then can we begin to dismantle it, see how it works, and create procedures to nullify it.

The limiting mind may present hindering voices, images, or physical feelings when it's time to approach strangers and make their acquaintance. Let's identify the types of internal media it can use to intimidate you into aborting a social mission.

Voices of the limiting mind include:

- **Self-doubt:** "You won't know what to say" or "Remember last time you messed up?"
- **Other-oriented doubt:** "She probably has a boyfriend," "She wouldn't be interested in me," or "She's busy and I'd be interrupting her."
- **Environmental doubt:** "Everyone around will make fun of me" or "It's too loud for her to hear me."
- **Existential rationalization:** "Why bother? It won't work out anyway," "I don't feel like it right now," or "I'm having too much fun with my friends."
- **False judgments:** "She isn't attractive enough" or "She seems way too shallow for me."

Images of the limiting mind include getting ignored; being mocked or bullied; being sad and alone; being observed and judged; getting beaten up; being rejected; and seeing more qualified or successful men in the room.

The limiting mind also expresses itself through physical sensations. When a potential threat registers on your radar, the acute stress response (also known as the fight-or-flight response) releases adrenaline into your system. This hormone increases your breathing and heart rate; constricts blood vessels; tenses muscles; dilates pupils; elevates your blood sugar level; and weakens your immune system.

Awaken Your Freedom Mind

To abolish approach anxiety, convince yourself logically that the dialogue of your limiting mind is incorrect and in fact self-sabotaging. In your Day 1 reading assignment, several limiting beliefs were disproven. These are the kinds of rational responses your freedom mind can use when the limiting mind rears its ugly head.

For example, if your limiting mind tells you, "She won't hear you," your freedom mind should answer back, "If she doesn't hear me the first time, I'll smile and politely repeat myself more loudly, slowly, and clearly."

If your limiting mind tells you that you're going to get nervous, your freedom mind can say, "I may have a natural stress reaction to this situation because, after all, it is somewhat stressful. But that doesn't mean I won't be able to push through it. In the past, nervousness has given me the energy I needed to perform at my best and feel good about myself. So let's do this!"

Take a moment to write down your own limiting mind's reservations about approaching. Then write down corresponding freedom mind responses that empower you. Use the word *you* for the scripts of your limiting mind, and the words *I* and *me* in your freedom mind responses. This will help you disassociate from your limiting mind and associate more closely with your freedom mind.

It's up to you to feed positive scripts into your freedom mind on a regular basis, to give it the power to overcome, persevere, and succeed. To do this, pick three freedom mind scripts or affirmations that you feel would best replace your specific fears, whether they're the ones you just wrote down or ones included in this book. Write them on a single sheet of paper. Then read them out loud with conviction during your morning or evening freedom mind ritual, and run them through your mind over the course of the day. Once you start to feel the beneficial changes, switch to another set of affirmations according to your new needs.

Shift Your Submodalities

Submodalities are the media through which your senses receive, remember, and process information. For example, auditory submodalities include volume, pitch, tempo, and timbre.

To help eliminate negative internal dialogue, try adjusting the submodalities of your limiting mind's voice. Make it quieter and further away; stammering and squeaky; or use the voice of a person you don't like.

At the same time, give your freedom mind a strong, low-pitched, calm, nearby voice. Consider making it the voice of someone you respect: a mentor, an actor, or your future best self.

If these exercises seem at first glance like New Age tripe, that's your limiting mind at work again. This process is exactly what trainers instruct top athletes to do to master their game. It's also one way that therapists eliminate phobias.

Visually, put your mental pictures and movies through the same filters. First, overpower the images of failure in your limiting mind with the successful images of your freedom mind. Change a picture of getting ignored to one of being adored; change a picture of being rejected into a bright, vivid visualization of a beautiful woman pressing her phone number into your palm.

Now change the submodalities. Make the images in your limiting mind small, distant, black-and-white, slow-moving, blurry, and dark. Disassociate with these negative images by seeing them not through your own eyes but as if you're watching yourself as a character on a movie screen.

Whenever your limiting mind images pop up, instantly replace them with large, bright, sharp, colorful pictures of successful situations. Associate with these images by seeing them through your own eyes.

These mental exercises are best done just after waking up or before going to sleep, because that's when your subconscious is most open to changework. By repeating this exercise as often as possible, you'll get to the point where you automatically reject the negative images your limiting mind tries to throw at you before each approach.

Let Go of Your Outcome

One of the biggest problems men have with approaching women is magnifying the meaning of the interaction and focusing too intently on achieving one specific outcome—whether it be exchanging phone numbers, making out, having sex, or beginning a romantic relationship.

Emotionally detaching from the outcome—while rationally working toward your goal—will significantly alleviate your anxiety. This is why the Stylelife Challenge offers small, easy-to-accomplish goals rather than large, unlikely ones.

People can be random, unpredictable, chaotic creatures. And sometimes you may truly be surprised. That's why approaching is so much fun. So why constrain the possibilities of a new encounter by being dependent on a particular outcome?

Remove Failure from Your Vocabulary

The word *failure* has different meanings for different people. To most people, failure means approaching and being rejected. My definition of failure is quitting, giving up, or never approaching at all.

Rejection is another word that's been misused and misrepresented. The dictionary definition of *reject* is "to refuse to accept." So if you offer someone a stick of gum, and she says "No thanks," you've been rejected. Do you feel an emotional sting? Probably not.

If you invite someone to a social event, and she says "No thanks," it shouldn't be any different. But for most people it is different, and here's why: When the gum is rejected, we think the person doesn't want the gum. But when we extend an invitation and get rejected, we think she doesn't want us.

But how could she possibly have decided she doesn't want us? She's known us only for a short while. She's practically a complete stranger. She doesn't know how great we are, the way our friends and family do. Why do we value her opinion over theirs? Why do we attach so much emotional baggage to a virtual stranger's ill-formed opinion? You guessed it: the limiting mind.

Practice the Crash and Burn Strategy

If, after reading this, you still have a crippling fear of social rejection, then go out and try to get rejected. Every accomplished social artist I know has a ton of rejections under his belt. That's simply the price you have to pay for excellence.

To quote Michael Jordan, "I've missed more than nine thousand shots in my career. I've lost almost three hundred games. Twenty-six times, I've been trusted to take the game-winning shot and missed. I've failed over and over and over again in my life. And that is why I succeed."

After a few rejections, you'll see that it's not so bad, that rejection really has nothing to do with who you are. It's more like somebody flicking you in the shoulder with a finger. You know it happened, but it doesn't hurt you or really even bother you. It's actually just immature and embarrassing on their part.

I took a student out once and tried to get us rejected to help him past his fears. But a funny thing happened: My plan backfired, and I wasn't rejected at all. The conversation went something like this:

ME: Hey! How are you doing? Could you blow us out? We need to get blown out.

THEM: Huh? What's that?

ME: Oh, that's when a couple of guys roll up and you're in some mood, so you're totally rude and don't wanna talk, and you tell the guys to—

THEM [*INTERRUPTING*]: Oh, we're not rude. Not at all!

We ended up having a pleasant conversation for forty-five minutes, after which we exchanged contact information. The exercise was supposed to demonstrate that blow-outs are pain free, but it ended up teaching a different lesson: that you can open by saying almost anything when you're confident, congruent, and upbeat.

Feel free to prove it to yourself. Next time you see someone you want to talk to, open your mouth and say the first thing that comes to mind. As long as your comment or question isn't rude or hostile, you may be surprised by how difficult it is to get solidly rejected.

After trying this a few times, you'll also notice that everyone's responses vary. Then you can adjust your attitude to expect nothing and prepare for everything. Or, as the poet Samuel Hazo puts it:

> *Expect everything, and anything seems nothing.*
> *Expect nothing, and anything seems everything.*

STOP!

· ·

DID YOU COMPLIMENT FOUR WOMEN?
DID YOU SHOP FOR NEW CLOTHES?
DID YOU CREATE YOUR MISSION STATEMENT,
DO THE POSTURE EXERCISE, GET MOVIE RECOMMENDATIONS
FROM THREE STRANGERS?

IF YOU ANSWERED YES TO ALL OF THESE QUESTIONS, THEN
PROCEED TO THE NEXT PAGE.

IF YOU HAVEN'T ACTUALLY BEEN DOING THE MISSIONS
BUT JUST READING TO GET THE INFORMATION,
THEN DO NOT PROGRESS PAST THIS PAGE UNTIL YOU CAN
ANSWER YES TO THE QUESTIONS ABOVE.

READING THIS WORKBOOK STRAIGHT THROUGH
IS LIKE GOING TO THE GYM TO WATCH TELEVISION.
YOU'RE NOT GOING TO IMPROVE
IF YOU DON'T DO THE EXERCISES.

DAY

7

MISSION 1: Learn to Open

Your first lesson today: There is no such thing as a pickup line.

If there were a single sentence that magically made women fall in love or lust, every man would be using it. Most of what people call pickup lines are actually comedic one-liners that were never legitimately used to meet women in the first place.

What does exist is a specific sequential process that can be used to develop a romantic or sexual relationship with a woman.

And this process begins with the opener, perhaps the most important part of the interaction.

Your task is to turn to your Day 7 Briefing and read the field guide to openers before beginning the next mission.

MISSION 2: Prepare Your Opener

Your mission is to develop an original opener based on today's briefing.

The simplest way to generate an opener is to think about anything you're curious about, want to learn, or are confused about. Choose a topic that is likely to capture the interest of most people. It can be a meaningful, debate-inspiring subject based on a relationship or spiritual crisis, or it can be a specific, trivial subject based on a popular culture, travel, health, or social customs query.

Then, instead of asking a friend about the subject or looking up the information on the internet, use it as a reason to talk to other people. For example, if you can't remember who sings a certain popular song, make it your mission when you leave the house today to ask strangers until you get a correct answer.

If your friend's girlfriend tried to kiss you, and you don't know whether to tell him or not, by all means, get some advice from the woman in the street.

Even unlikely questions can be effective openers as long as they're genuine. For example, I was having a debate with a friend one day over the names of the oceans. So, rather than seek the immediate gratification of Google, we made it our opener for the night: "Hey, how good were you at high school geography? Okay, how many continents are there? Right, seven. And how many oceans? Okay, five. So here's the question: What are the five oceans? My friend and I have been stuck on this all day. We can come up with only four."

As ridiculous as it sounds, it started a conversation every time.

Although today's briefing mentions different types of openers, for this task, focus on indirect openers that don't convey sexual or romantic interest. Make sure your attitude about whatever you ask is positive and that you avoid discussing anything that might reflect badly on you, such as creepy topics like serial killers or insecure questions about yourself.

MISSION 3: Test Your Opener

Get groomed, get dressed, and get excited. Your mission today is to approach three different women—or groups that include women—and deliver either an opener you've invented or one you read in today's material. You may approach in the street, at a café or bar, in the mall, in an office waiting room, or wherever you choose.

It isn't necessary to continue the conversation afterward, but feel free to do so if it's going well. When the discussion comes to a natural close, exit with a simple line: "Thanks. Nice meeting you," for example.

It is not necessary to have three successful interactions; just three approaches. Tomorrow we'll add a few extra pieces that will greatly increase the success and effectiveness of your openers.

MISSION 4: Evaluate Your Approaches

In the space below, make a list of the approaches you did today.

If any went well, write down the reasons you believe they worked. If any went poorly, make a note of why you believe they weren't successful.

Approach #1:

_____

_____

_____

_____

Approach #2:

_____

_____

_____

_____

Approach #3:

_____

_____

_____

_____

Now review your list. Do any of your reasons blame someone else for a negative outcome ("She was walking too fast," "She was stuck up," "She wasn't my type," "The guy she was with was an asshole")? If so, cross them out and replace them with an error you may have made. Then write down a suggestion for what you could have done differently to make the approach more successful.

DAY 7 BRIEFING
A FIELD GUIDE TO OPENERS

"What's your name?" "What do you do for work?" "Seen any good movies lately?"

Boring!

Listen to any man in conversation with a woman he's met, and chances are she'll be subjected to a nonstop barrage of questions that include one or all of the above. And because she's answering them, the guy will think he's getting somewhere.

Here's a question for you: How many times do you think she's answered those same questions before?

Answer: countless times.

Usually, the scenario ends like this: Slowly she starts looking around the bar, losing interest. The guy makes a desperate move and asks for her phone number. She politely says she has a boyfriend, even though she doesn't. Game over.

Why does this happen?

The comedian Chris Rock knows why. He has a routine in which he explains that anything a man says to a woman translates as "How about some dick?"

If you barrage a woman with generic questions, what she hears is "How about some dick?" Offer to buy her a drink, she hears "How about some dick?" Introduce yourself to her, comment on her necklace, ask for the time: "How about some dick?"

Your goal as a Challenger is to start a conversation with a woman without saying "How about some dick?"

This is accomplished through what are known as indirect openers. An indirect opener is a way to start a conversation with a stranger or a group of people you don't know without hitting on anyone or showing any romantic interest. If you do this well enough, soon she'll be asking *you* those generic questions.

The following guide includes the basics of using and developing these openers. Tomorrow, you'll learn two additional techniques to make them nearly failsafe.

Types of Openers

A successful opener serves four basic objectives:

- It's nonthreatening and makes no one uncomfortable.
- It stirs up curiosity and captures the person's or group's imagination.
- It's a springboard for follow-up conversation.
- It serves as a vehicle for you to display your personality.

There are many different types and classes of openers. These include:

- Direct openers, in which the man shows his romantic or sexual interest right away;

- Situational openers, in which the man comments on something in the environment;
- Indirect openers, in which the man initiates a spontaneous, entertaining conversation that is not about the woman or the environment.

All of these openers can work, but the first two often fall into the "How about some dick?" category. It's okay to use them, but only if the woman is initially interested in you or predisposed to be attracted to you. And even then they may not always work.

I prefer indirect openers because, when performed correctly, they work 95 percent of the time. And those are pretty good odds in this game, or any game.

Most indirect openers are premeditated and scripted. It may seem contrived and unnatural to prepare something to say, but when you have a conversation starter ready to go at any time, you don't have to hesitate and try to think of something clever to say every time you see a woman you find attractive.

Eventually you'll be able to start a successful interaction by spontaneously saying just about anything. For now, though, think of indirect scripted openers as training wheels—ones that work so well many guys never want to remove them.

Before the Opener

The game begins before you open your mouth.

Because the initial approach is such a critical moment, everything from your body language to your energy level takes on extra significance. Here are a few points to keep in mind when approaching a woman or a group of strangers:

- Always have something better to do than meeting women. As soon as you start staring at, evaluating, or ogling a woman in front of you, even if she can't see you, you've just lost every woman behind you. The reason is not just that you may seem creepy and desperate, but also that you don't seem interesting, fun, or worth meeting.
- Everyone wants to be with the most popular person in the room.

Since most groups in public settings don't know each other, all you need to do is create the illusion of being popular in that moment. From the second you walk in, be engrossed in an animated conversation with your friends. Smile, laugh, have fun, and enjoy one another's company.

■ Then, when you notice someone you want to approach, wheel around and start a conversation. Don't hesitate or waste time assessing the situation. The art of the approach is the art of spontaneity. If you wait too long, either she'll notice you scoping her out and get creeped out—or, more likely, you'll think about it for too long, get nervous, and talk yourself out of approaching.

■ Don't face the person or group head-on when you first approach. It's too direct and confrontational. Instead, turn your head and ask over your shoulder. Your goal is to give the impression that you're on your way somewhere else and just pausing briefly to ask some random people a quick question en route. Once the group begins to enjoy the conversation, you may turn and face them.

■ Don't hover over or lean into the person or group. If you're competing with loud music or they're seated, just stand up straighter and talk louder. If all goes well, you'll soon be sitting down with them or moving somewhere quieter together.

■ Smile when you approach. Even if a grin doesn't come naturally, fake it. It predisposes the woman or group you're about to engage to respond positively. On a subconscious level, it signals that you're a friend and not an enemy.

■ Your energy level should be equal to or slightly higher than the woman or group you're approaching. Most people are out to have fun. So if you can add to their fun, you'll be welcomed into the group. If you're bringing them down or making them strain to understand you, it doesn't matter what you say—they'll want to get rid of you as soon as possible. Ways to increase your energy level include talking louder, using hand gestures, making an effort to connect with the people you're talking to, and smiling with your mouth and eyes. But don't be too hyper, because that's just annoying.

■ Make sure that everyone can hear you, is paying attention, and is involved in the conversation. If you lose just one person, you risk losing the whole group. So if you feel like someone's interest is waning, pull her into the conversation by addressing her directly or commenting on something she's wearing or doing.

■ Don't be afraid to approach groups that include men. The more men there are in the group, the less likely it is that the women in it have been approached. You'll be surprised at how often the guys they're with aren't actually their boyfriends or husbands.

■ Make sure you pay attention to the men in a group. If they feel you're not respecting or acknowledging them, they'll try to end the interaction. If you think any of the men mistakenly believe you're hitting on them, mention an ex-girlfriend or a crush on an actress.

■ If you're interested in an attractive woman or group of women who've been hit on a lot, don't approach them directly. Instead, open a group next to them. Then, during a high point of the interaction, casually involve the woman you originally wanted to meet in the discussion.

What to Say

There are three traits a successful indirect opener should possess: It should appear spontaneous, be motivated by curiosity, and be interesting to most people.

There are also many subtleties. Never begin by asking a question that requires a yes or no response. If you say, "Can I ask you a quick question?" the group can always answer, "No." Then you're stuck.

Instead, begin with a statement, such as an observation, "You guys look like experts," or a request for assistance: "Help me settle a quick debate" or "Let me get your take on this." Then pause briefly to make sure you have everyone's attention, and continue.

Even when you ask your actual question, it's not necessary to get an answer. Pause for a moment, and if no one fills in the silence with an opinion, continue with your story.

Don't begin the opener by saying "I'm sorry," "Excuse me," or "Pardon me, but." Sure, your family raised you to be polite, but starting a conversation this way makes you sound insecure at best and like a panhandler at worst. Where men are initially attracted to beauty, most women are initially attracted to status. And a man of high status never apologizes for his presence.

The most widely used kind of indirect opener I've come up with is the opinion opener, in which you ask a group for advice on a personal story. A well camouflaged opinion opener can still evoke ten minutes of excited responses—which are also ten minutes you can use to showcase your humor and personality.

An easy opener for beginners is the "shady friend opener," which was based on a girl I dated. One bonus with this routine is that it can help you ascertain if the girl you're interested in is too jealous to seriously date.

Here's a word-for-word script. It was originally created in bars and clubs, so if you're out by yourself during the day, instead of pointing to a friend in the room, pretend you just got off the phone with him.

> YOU: Hey guys, let me get your take on something. I'm trying to give my friend over there advice, but we're just a bunch of men—so we're not really qualified to comment on these matters.
>
> THEM: What's that?
>
> YOU: Okay, this is a two-part question. If you've been dating a guy for three months and he doesn't want you to hang out with one of your male friends, what's the appropriate response? Assuming that the person is just your friend, and nothing would ever happen.
>
> THEM: I'd probably break up with the guy I'm dating.
>
> YOU: Okay, here's the second part of the question. What if this friend was someone you used to sleep with? Does that change things?
>
> THEM: Well, I'm friends with some of my exes, but others I can't be friends with. So it depends.
>
> YOU: Okay, makes sense. The reason I'm asking is because my friend over there has been dating a girl for three months, and she wants him to stop talking to a female friend of his. He hasn't dated this other girl for years, and they're really just friends. The problem is, if he stops talking to her, he'll resent his girlfriend. But if he keeps talking to her, his girlfriend will resent him.
>
> THEM: Something like that happened to me once, and . . .

If you're talking to a group, make sure you ask all the members—even the men—for their opinions. No one should be excluded, because if they are, they'll feel slighted or get bored—and could influence the group to shut you out.

Most important, as you deliver this or any other opener, remember that it's not the exact words that matter—it's your attitude. The opener is used only to break the ice and get the group's attention. It contains no magic formula that will make a woman swoon at your feet. It's just a way to keep your mouth moving while you display your charming personality.

After the Opener

A good opener will naturally lead to other questions and topics of conversation.

Often, you'll be asked for your take on the dilemma you've asked about. Make sure you have one. If you're normally a sarcastic or negative person, this worldview may create a bond with some women, but it rarely creates attraction. I know because I used to be that way, until I discovered that one of the keys to drawing people to you—and making them want to stay there—is radiating positivity.

This is why it's best to draw openers from your own life. If the opener is about someone in college, you should know what college it is. If it's about someone in another country, you should know what country it is. Determine in advance the ages, professions, relationships, and other details of the people in the openers you use. If you deliver the opener correctly, she will most likely be curious and ask follow-up questions. So be prepared.

But don't overprepare. You'll come up with plenty of clever responses to common questions, related topics to discuss, and interesting details in the moment. For example, if you're using the shady friend opener, and it elicits a flurry of conflicting opinions, you may find yourself saying, with a bemused smile, "You guys are great. You're just like *The View*."

However, beware of a common beginner mistake: milking the opener. As soon as the energy starts to flag, or you catch yourself thinking too hard of something to say to continue the conversation, the opener is over. Cut the thread and move on.

You'll learn exactly what to say next in future Challenge assignments, but for now just remember: As soon as you start struggling to keep a dying conversation topic going, you may as well be asking "How about some dick?"

The Rule of Trying

Now that you're learning scripted material, it's important to remember the rule of trying: *Don't*. If you try hard, you die hard.

As soon as you're caught trying to impress her, trying to get validation, trying for attention, or trying too hard in any way, the game is over. One of the paradoxes of the game is that it takes a lot of effort to appear effortless.

While it's possible that in the future certain routines and lines in this book may become well known, the principles upon which they work have always been and will always be true. So feel free at any point to go to www.stylelife.com/challenge to learn new and proven openers created by Challengers and coaches.

As you become more advanced, you'll find yourself relying less on pre-scripted openers. You'll eventually be able to go out with friends and challenge one another to come up with the most ridiculous opening lines possible. And as long as your attitude is upbeat, non-needy, empathic, and positive, you'll discover that you can do no wrong.

Troubleshooting

Tomorrow you'll learn the two keys to avoiding most things that can go wrong during an opener.

For now, just remember that whatever happens during the opener is feedback. A rejection is not a comment on you but on your technique.

If a woman tells you that she has a boyfriend (and you haven't asked), it means she thought you were hitting on her. If she says she has to go to the bathroom, it means you made her uncomfortable. Adjust your future approaches based on these responses and develop answers that will transform common objections into attraction-building material. For example, if she accuses you of using a pickup line, you can respond, "You thought I was hitting on you? That's cute, but I don't think you could handle me."

Whatever you do, always remember the golden rule: You must open.

If you don't approach, you'll never know whether that stranger could have become a girlfriend, a casual fling, a good friend, or even a career opportunity. Almost every student I've talked with has regrets about not approaching a girl. But few have ever regretted making an approach, no matter what happened.

The pain of letting yourself down is much greater than anything someone else can say.

DAY

8

MISSION 1: Fine-tune Your Openers

Congratulations on delivering your first openers. Some of you may have found that conversations began with ease. Others, not so much. If you felt like you were bugging people, if someone asked whether you were taking a survey, or if you got funny looks, that doesn't mean you did anything wrong. It just means you're ready for your next mission.

Today you're going to learn two key subtleties of opening. Once you add these pieces to your approach, you'll notice a big difference in the effectiveness of the opener and the responses you get.

So turn to your Day 8 Briefing and read about the two keys before continuing to the next mission.

MISSION 2: Approach with Your New Tools

Approach three women—or groups that include women—with the opener you used yesterday.

This time, add both a root and a time constraint to each approach.

MISSION 3: Evaluate

When you return home, ask yourself if there was anything different about the responses you received from women you approached today, compared with those you approached yesterday. List three differences in the space below:

_____

_____

_____

_____

If you used an opener you made up, but it didn't seem to spark a natural conversation, then in future missions try using one of the scripts provided in this book (such as the shady friend or five oceans openers), or examine and modify your opener.

If you're not sure whether your opener is effective, post it on the Stylelife website message boards. There your fellow Challengers will evaluate and, if necessary, strengthen the material.

DAY 8 BRIEFING
THE TWO KEYS

As soon as you approach a group of strangers, they generally think two things: "What does this person want from me?" and "How long is he going to stay here?"

One of the strategies of the game is anticipating and defusing these objections—and any objections—before they happen. If you do this successfully in the first minute or two of your approach, you'll be much less likely to receive negative or flat responses.

Rooting

If a woman doesn't know why you're talking to her, she'll generally be suspicious until she either finds out from you or guesses her own reason. This is why people using opinion openers for the first time are often asked if they're taking a survey.

To anticipate the question "What does this person want from me?" you need to "root" your opener by giving your question a legitimate context.

For example, the opener may be something that's just now come up in your life, and there's a slightly urgent need to get an answer immediately.

The best way to convey this is to explain at some point during the opener why you're asking. You can use the following words to introduce your root: "The reason I'm asking is because . . ."

In the shady friend opener, the reason you're asking is that your buddy just moved in with his girlfriend, and she doesn't want him to talk to one of his female friends. And you were just now trying to give him advice, but he won't listen and you need some backup.

The root doesn't always need to be elaborate. It can be as simple as: "My friend and I were just talking, and we need a woman's perspective." If you're not with a friend, then it can be a discussion you were just having on your cell phone. Anything reasonable qualifies as a root, as long as it lets the woman or group know why you walked up and started talking to them about that particular subject at that very moment.

Time Constraints

For most inexperienced men, the game consists of approaching a woman and trying to stay in constant conversation until she either dismisses him or sleeps with him. Because of this, women have developed a vast array of tactics to get rid of guys who lurk too long.

This is why, from now on, you're going to let her know right away that you're not one of those guys. Unless she's already attracted to you, from the minute you approach she will most likely be wondering how to get rid of you. Her strategies for doing so may include telling you she's in the middle of an important conversation with her friends, claiming she has to go to the bathroom, or pretending that she has a boyfriend or is a lesbian.

So to anticipate the question "How long is he going to stay here?" you'll need to use a time constraint.

A time constraint is anything that explicitly lets the woman or group know that you don't plan on hanging around long. It should be inserted in the first minute of conversation, before the group has the chance to wonder when your story is going to end. So preface the opener you've been using with a time constraint like, "I have to get back to my friend in a minute, but, really quickly . . ." Or, in the middle of your opener, explain, "By the way, it's guys night out and I shouldn't even be talking to you all."

A time constraint doesn't have to be verbal. It can be physical as well. This is conveyed by leaning away, rocking on your back foot, taking a few steps away as you're talking, or anything else that makes it look like you're in a hurry or on your way somewhere else.

The best time constraints contain both elements: They're expressed verbally and sold through body language.

When you use both a time constraint and a root, it allows the woman or group to stop worrying about what you want and how to get rid of you, and relax enough to listen to what you have to say.

But wait, you may be thinking. If you just told her you have to leave in a minute, how are you supposed to keep talking to her after the opener?

Good question.

The next key stage of the interaction is known as the "hook point." This is when, instead of being a stranger taking up her time, you've captivated her—and suddenly she doesn't want you to leave. So, reluctantly, you allow her to take up a little more of your precious time.

Becoming that guy is what the next week of the Stylelife Challenge is all about.

DAY

9

MISSION 1: Crunch Time

Next week, the pace is going to pick up. So to make sure you're caught up and ready to proceed, today is review day.

Your task is to look over the previous eight days of assignments. Then ask yourself:

- Is there any mission I skipped?
- Is there any mission I feel I didn't complete?
- Is there any mission I didn't perform to my satisfaction?
- Is there any mission I'd like to do again?
- Have I backslid in my vocal training, posture, grooming, or commitment to my goals?

Take this opportunity to explore or repeat any previous assignments and exercises you need to reinforce.

MISSION 2: Approach Mixed Groups

If you've approached only lone women or groups of women during the Challenge so far, then it's time to approach groups that contain men.

Your mission is to approach two groups of three or more people that include men as well as women.

Approaching groups with men may sound daunting if you haven't done it yet, but it's generally easier in practice. The more intimidating people are to approach, the less likely it is they've been approached.

Don't forget, all you have to do to ensure the success of the approach is make sure that the guys are always involved in the conversation, they feel respected, and they know you're not hitting on the women. At least not yet.

MISSION 3: Intervention

Statistically, the ninth day of a new self-improvement program is the point when most people drop out. That's not going to be you. So your final task today is to read your Day 9 Briefing and prepare to learn how to learn.

DAY 9 BRIEFING
THE FOURTEEN LAWS OF LEARNING

When I first set off on my journey to learn the game, a college junior named Chad emailed me. He had discovered the world of pickup artistry six months earlier and was already well versed in the basic concepts. However, he was still a virgin.

He was far better looking than I was, with a stocky build, wavy black hair, and a square jaw. Yet a year later, I was having fantastic adventures that I'd never thought were possible for a guy like me. And Chad, despite working just as hard, was still a virgin. So I sat down with him one night and tried to figure out why. The reason, we eventually realized, was that we had different strategies for learning.

Afterward, I began developing the fourteen laws of learning that follow. They apply not just to the game, but to school, work, and hobbies. They are what separate a chump who's banging his head against the wall in frustration from a champ who's smoothly ascending to the top of the game. Make sure you understand and can practice each principle before moving on to the next.

1. **Acquire and apply knowledge in small chunks.** Some people are perfect preparers. They want to gather every scrap of information on a subject before taking action. And though they seem to be working hard, this is actually a form of procrastination. The best way to learn the game is to take it one step at a time. Just learn what you need to get to the next level. If you can't approach women, just work

on openers. When you master openers, then learn how to continue the conversation. Don't worry about advanced sexual techniques. You'll soon get there if you continue to progress by adding one piece at a time as you need it.

2. **There is no such thing as rejection, only feedback.** A lot of people get discouraged and give up after a single setback or rejection. They tend to take rejection personally, seeing it as a comment on who they are rather than what it really is: feedback on what they're doing. Every time you approach a group of people and something goes wrong, you've been presented with an opportunity to learn why they responded negatively and what you could have done to prevent that. If you possess the ability to learn from your mistakes, then failure is literally impossible, because each rejection brings you closer to perfection.

3. **It's never her fault.** Who do you blame when something goes wrong during an approach? If you catch yourself saying that a situation was impossible, the guys were jerks, or the woman was just a "bitch," then you're wrong. It was your fault. It's always your fault. And that's a good thing, because it means you're in control. So never blame any person or situation. Instead, demonstrate a willingness to examine yourself and accept criticism *without taking it personally*. Only then can you accurately determine whether there was something you could have done to change the outcome, or if the outcome was truly unavoidable.

4. **Learn actively rather than passively.** Just as you can't learn to play football by watching videos and posting in football newsgroups, the only way to learn to attract women is from real-world experience. Anyone can sit in a seminar or buy a DVD and learn the principles, but the guys who win the game are the ones who can apply them.

5. **Don't rehearse negative outcomes.** One of the biggest problems men have when it comes to meeting women is that they re

hearse negative scenarios in their minds. Often, these become excuses not to go out and try something new. Instead, get out of the house, make a few approaches, and if any of these scenarios happens to occur in real life, *then* find out what to do. This isn't skydiving: There's little to no risk of actual harm from being unprepared.

6. **Understand how your mind learns.** The psychological field of neurolinguistic programming (NLP) offers a useful four-step model of how the mind learns. It can serve as a yardstick to measure your progress.

   ■ *Unconscious incompetence:* You're doing something wrong, and you don't even know you're doing it wrong.

   ■ *Conscious incompetence:* You're doing something wrong, and you're aware that you're doing it wrong, but you haven't yet fixed the problem.

   ■ *Conscious competence:* You've learned the right way to do it, and you're doing it correctly with focused attention.

   ■ *Unconscious competence:* You no longer have to think about something or work on learning it—you automatically do it correctly. In the parlance of the game, this is when you finally become a so-called natural.

7. **Be willing to go through the pain period.** This game is not an easy one. You'll be forced to confront nearly every single thing that defines you—every emotion, every action, every belief. You'll sometimes be apprehensive about approaching a particular woman, trying a new technique, or changing a behavior. What separates an amateur from a champion is the willingness to push through that fear and do it anyway. Here's what Arnold Schwarzenegger, in his iron-pumping days, had to say about it: "If you can go through the pain period, you make it to be a champion. If you can't go through it, forget it. And that's what most people lack: having the guts—the guts to go in and just say . . . 'I don't care what happens.' "

8. **Don't look to friends or family for approval.** Not all of your friends and family will understand the journey you're about to take.

They may tell you that they don't like how you're changing. They may make fun of you for wanting to improve. That's okay. It happened to me. It also happened to Oprah: When she lost weight, she lost friends. This surprised her at first, until she learned that her largeness had given them an excuse to feel better about their own bodies. So, when you start attracting women and adventure, your friends may not welcome it—you've become a threat to their limiting beliefs and complacency about their own shortcomings. Let it be their problem, not yours.

9. **Be willing to test new ideas, even if they don't seem logical.** Before I learned the game, I considered myself an intelligent and successful person. Yet the logic that had gotten me so far in the world wasn't getting me anywhere with women. In order to make a change, I had to try some new behaviors, even if they didn't seem logical. I said things I thought would drive women away, but instead they attracted them. I wore outrageous clothes I thought would get me laughed out of the room, but instead they motivated women to approach me. And that's when I realized that I'd never really been using logic in the first place—because, as any good scientist knows, before dismissing a new hypothesis, it's necessary to test it first.

10. **Once something works, figure out how and why it works.** There are some men who do great just following these instructions and repeating the routines. But the ones who become superstars are the ones who, after a series of successes, figure out *why* the routines worked and what made them work. There's only one rule of pickup, and that rule is: There are no rules, only guidelines. Once you understand the principles behind each idea, you'll know when to follow the guidelines, when to dismiss them, and when to invent new ones.

11. **If you don't know what to do, don't leave.** If you run out of material when talking to a woman you've just met, you're not going to learn anything by running away. Stay in the conversation and, if you run out of things to say, push it five, ten, twenty minutes fur-

ther—even if you have to violate the guidelines and buy her a drink or ask interview questions. It's the best way to learn something new for next time.

12. **Hang around someone better than yourself.** This is the single best way to improve in any area. Your mentor doesn't have to be the top attraction expert in the world, just someone who has a little more skill than you do. If you don't know anyone who can fill this role, instead of going out to meet women one night, go out to befriend someone who's good with women.

13. **Make sure that your ratio of effort to results is increasing.** When learning a new way of doing something, most people get worse at the task before getting better. That's normal. But you'd be surprised by the number of people who keep putting more work into something after this transition period, even though their results stay the same or barely improve. So make sure you're increasing not just your knowledge but also your results. If you're not, then take a break, review these rules, examine what you're doing, and push yourself beyond your comfort zone.

14. **Finish what you begin.** Most people can accomplish just about anything within the realm of possibility. Despite this, they never realize their dreams. Either they quit before they reach their goals (and always with a seemingly good reason for doing so), or they don't change their strategy when something's not working. Roughly 19 out of 20 people who start reading this book won't stick with the program until the end. Don't be one of those people. Simply by not giving up, you'll already be in the top 5 percent of men out there.

DAY
10

MISSION 1: It's Opposite Day

The focus of today's lesson is disqualification—one of the most counterintuitive techniques in the Stylelife Challenge. Forget everything you know about attracting women, because the goal of disqualification is to meet women and tell them you *don't* want to date them.

This is going to be the most difficult day of the Challenge so far—but also the most rewarding. To find out what it's all about, read your Day 10 Briefing and fill out the worksheet describing your ideal woman.

MISSION 2: Play Hard to Get

Your mission today is to make three approaches using one of the openers you've learned or created.

During the first approach, add a disqualifier from today's reading material.

For the second approach, use a different disqualifier.

Afterward, take a short break and think of a third potential way to disqualify her. Write it below:

_____

_____

_____

_____

Now make your third approach and, during the opener, use the disqualifier you just invented.

DAY 10 BRIEFING
THE POWER OF NO

It's not the having, it's the getting.
—ELIZABETH TAYLOR

I recently went to a party in Colorado with six friends. Three of the guys spent the night with women; three didn't. As we discussed it the next morning, we discovered that the difference between the unsuccessful guys and the successful guys boiled down to one thing: lack of neediness.

The guys who went home alone were too available. The successful guys all played hard to get. They weren't afraid to walk away from the woman they were attracted to, talk to other people at the party, and create the impression that if she didn't act soon, she'd lose her chance. They understood a basic tenet of human nature: The harder we have to work for something, the more we value it.

Thus the lesson for today: In every interaction, be the person *giving* validation, not the one needing it.

One of the quickest and most playful ways to accomplish this is through disqualification. To disqualify a woman, demonstrate early in an interaction that you're not interested in her. Even though you may be chasing her, disqualification turns the tables and makes her want to chase you. For example, telling a woman with blonde hair that for some reason you've only dated brunettes disqualifies her as a potential girlfriend.

If the concept sounds odd, consider this: Beautiful women are constantly approached by men. They assume that nearly every guy wants to sleep with them. So when you take yourself out of the dating pool in a confident way, you immediately stand out—after all, most people want what they can't have.

Another advantage is that disqualifying a woman in a group can help you win over her friends, who are used to repelling the steady stream of men vying for her attention.

Finally, disqualification helps build trust because it demonstrates that you're not solely motivated by the desire to sleep with her. By waiting before showing interest, you give her an opportunity to win you over with her charm, personality, and intelligence.

Not every relationship requires disqualification. Sometimes the feelings are mutual, and two people are attracted to each other right away. Also, if you're dealing with a woman whose confidence in her appeal is very low, you may want to avoid teasing her, since she's constantly disqualifying herself in her mind anyway.

Once you get comfortable using disqualifiers, you'll realize that they're not such a foreign, complex, counterintuitive concept at all, but in fact the bedrock of flirting.

Most disqualifiers are meant to be playful. Others are used to demonstrate that you have high standards and won't date or sleep with just anyone. However, a disqualifier should never be hostile, critical, judgmental, or condescending. There's a fine line between flirting and hurting. And disqualification is never intended to be mean or insulting. So say these with a smile on your face and laughter in your voice, as if you were good-naturedly picking on a younger sibling.

Screening

Women test men. They do so for many reasons: because they want to select the best potential mate from among many suitors; because they've been hurt in the past and don't want to make the same mistakes again; because they want confirmation that you authentically possess the qualities that attract them. Throughout your interactions with most women, whether they're consciously aware of it or not, they're putting you on the spot to see how you'll react.

These tests range from flirtatious teasing (such as telling a man he's too young or too old for her) to serious interview questions (such as asking a man why he and his last girlfriend broke up). Men normally sit there answering the questions like they're on a game show, hoping that if they accumulate enough points, she'll choose them. What they don't realize is that they're losing points simply by submitting to the test.

Screening allows you to flip the script and see if the woman you're interested in meets *your* standards. Before doing this, it's important to know exactly what your standards are.

Take a moment to imagine your ideal woman. Then list below five specific criteria you would like her to possess. Consider such qualities as personality, looks, upbringing, values, interests, knowledge, and life experience.

1. _____
2. _____
3. _____
4. _____
5. _____

Now list five deal breakers. Qualities that might prevent you from dating someone could include manipulativeness, narcissism, smoking, drinking, drug use, jealousy, pets you're allergic to, and emotional baggage.

1. _____
2. _____
3. _____
4. _____
5. _____

Keep in mind that this is just an exercise. When dating, remain open to the unexpected. If you're looking for someone who fits this bill exactly, you might overlook an even better match when she appears but doesn't meet your preset criteria.

In the meantime, this list will provide you with endless criteria for disqualification. On the simplest level, you can ask what her favorite films are and then act as if her answer is a deal breaker. "You actually liked that? That's it. I'm going home. Nice meeting you."

If you want someone who's adventurous, ask her: "What's the wildest, craziest thing you've ever done?" When she answers, disqualify her by saying, with a smile, "That's great. You and my grandma would really get along."

There's an endless list of potential criteria to screen her on, from her dancing skills to her preferred ice cream flavor to her lack of an Olympic gold medal (because you only date women with Olympic gold medals, so she'd better hurry up and get one).

The point of screening is never to make a woman feel bad about herself but to set yourself apart from the hordes of men who will sleep with anyone indiscriminately.

Push-Pull

The opposite of disqualification is qualification, or acceptance. When used together, these two techniques are very powerful.

If she says or does something good, give her a positive, accepting statement ("I like your attitude"); if she says something that could be perceived as negative, tease her with a disqualifier ("Note to self: Do not date this girl").

Taking control of an interaction by alternating back and forth between these two poles—punishment and reward, validation and invalidation, approval and disapproval, qualification and disqualification, push and pull—is one of the key ways to amplify attraction.

Like everything else in the game, push-pull should be doled out humorously and not cruelly. One way to make the process fun is to put her on a point system: Give her points for good behavior and subtract points for bad behavior. If you want to push it further, tell her that she can claim rewards at certain point thresholds: At forty points she gets to touch your bicep, at eighty she gets the first three digits of your phone number.

Perhaps the most fun form of push-pull is inventing a relationship prematurely. Tell her with a laugh that you're going to make her your girlfriend—on Fridays only—or joke that you're going to marry her on the spot. Then, moments later, pretend to be upset by something she just said or did and change the status of the relationship. Tell her you're demoting her to your Tuesday girlfriend, or you're filing for divorce and she can keep the cat.

10 More Ways to Disqualify

Disqualification can take myriad forms. Here are a few more to help with today's field assignment.

Remember, if you say these with a smile and a sense of humor, you'll come off as a great flirt. If you say them seriously, or as though you mean it, you're just an asshole.

- *Save her from you.* Often, trying to drive someone away is the best way to get her to chase you. Tell her you're the kind of guy her mother warned her about. Or say, "A good girl like you should probably be talking to a nice boy like that one over there." Not only does this make you seem fun and dangerous, but it inspires her to live up to that reputation as well.

■ *Give yourself a monetary value*. This can be done by pretending it's a privilege to talk to you or touch you. If she takes your hand, pull it away and joke, smiling, "Hey now, hands off the merchandise. That'll be forty dollars."

■ *Put her in the friend zone*. This is something women often do with men, but men rarely do with women. It can be done flirtatiously (by telling her she's like the little sister you never had), or more seriously, by telling her she'd make a great friend.

■ *Go over the top*. Exaggerate her greatness and pretend to be an awe-struck admirer. If you say this in a wry, superior way, you'll actually end up conveying the opposite.

■ *Reverse roles*. Everything she doesn't want a guy to do, jokingly accuse her of doing to you. Tell her to give her obvious pickup lines a rest, to stop treating you like a mindless piece of meat, to quit trying to get you drunk and take advantage of you because you're not that kind of guy. The more unlikely the scenario, the more effective your accusations.

■ *Employ her*. Jokingly offer to hire her as your assistant, your web designer, or some other job she'd never do. Then, of course, fire her moments later.

■ *Be the snob*. All those immature things the popular girls in school may have said to you, you may now say to her. Examples include: "Uhh, whatever," "Not so much," and "Yeah, you would say that."

■ *Be the authority figure*. The annoying things your parents and teachers told you are also fair game. Playfully tell her she's starting to get on your nerves, she's in big trouble, or she's just earned herself detention.

■ *Make her compete*. Threaten to leave to talk to your friends, the waitress, or those "more interesting girls over there."

■ *Challenge her:* Tell her you're not sure yet if she's cool enough, adventurous enough, or mature enough to hang out with you.

The list is endless. Any line a guy might use to hit on her, you should say the opposite. And anything she might say to a guy who's hitting on her, you can say to her instead.

It's that easy.

Performance Notes

For most of you, disqualifiers won't come easy—not because they're difficult, but because they go against everything you've been raised to say around women you like.

Tone is everything. Except for when you're actually screening someone to see if she meets your relationship criteria, most disqualifiers should be delivered playfully. If you appear serious or upset when you accuse her of hitting on you or not being cool enough for you, she'll think you're a psycho.

Most disqualifiers should also be delivered casually and offhand, as if you're not seeking or expecting a reaction. If it's obvious you're just using the disqualifer for effect, it loses its power and becomes just another form of neediness.

Though being rich, successful, and good-looking is normally a good thing when it comes to the game, it isn't with most disqualifiers. The point of the disqualifier is to raise your status to her level or above. But if she thinks your status is already far above hers, then most of these comments will make you sound obnoxiously arrogant rather than playfully cocky. So evaluate the situation before getting too hardcore with the material.

Finally, if you dish it out, be prepared to take it. She may respond to your disqualifier with a sharp comment of her own. If she does, don't panic. This a good thing. It's called flirting. Just be prepared with an even more clever retort to fire back. If you're stuck for an answer, just nod your head, smile, and say, "Respect," as if she's met your approval.

DAY

11

MISSION 1: Refine Your Identity

Today we're going to focus on the most important piece in the game: you.

In nearly every successful approach, at some point you'll be asked what you do. If you've mastered disqualifiers, your initial response will probably be to tease her for asking "interview questions" and then to claim to be a professional hopscotch player. If she persists, however, you're going to have to answer truthfully, or else she'll think you're hiding something.

The work question is an opportunity that most people waste. One student used to answer, "I'm an engineer." Engineering, of course, is a noble pursuit, but he felt like it made him sound boring to women.

When I asked him what he was working on, he said he was going to school to learn about new mobile phone technology. So we developed a better way for him to answer the question. Now, when women ask him what he does, he responds, "I'm designing the mobile phone of the future."

Same occupation, different identity.

In your Day 11 Briefing, there's an exercise that will help you refine your identity and articulate what you do in a crisp, compelling manner. Your mission is to fill it out and learn to succinctly express what makes you special without bragging.

MISSION 2: Approach and Continue

Approach groups of three or more people that include at least one woman. Use an opener that contains a time constraint and a root.

When you're finished with the opener, continue the conversation by adding the following movements and lines:

1. Pretend you're about to leave, but take no more than one step away.
2. Look back at the group and ask, out of curiosity, "Hey, how do you all know one another?"
3. Be ready to respond with a question or comment. It doesn't have to be anything clever or complex. If they say they're friends from work, ask, "So where do you all work?" If they say they're related, say, "That makes sense. I wonder which one of you is the black sheep."
4. You may now leave if you wish, with your all-purpose closer, "Nice meeting you."
5. You may also choose to continue talking to the group if the conversation is going well. If anyone asks what you do, answer with the identity statement you created today. Try to use the statement in at least one of your interactions.

The task is complete after you have followed steps 1 through 3 with three different groups of people.

MISSION 3: Master Your Inner Game

Too many of us have no idea what goes on inside our own heads. We don't understand our emotions, our passions, our frustrations, our needs, our thinking patterns, and why we sometimes act the way we do. And even when we do understand these things, we often find it difficult to change them.

One of the best books on this subject is *Mastering Your Hidden Self: A Guide to the Huna Way,* by an ex-marine named Serge Kahili King.

Though I recommend reading the entire book, for today's assignment I asked Stylelife senior coach Thomas Scott McKenzie to prepare a report summarizing its application to attraction. If your inner game needs a new set of rules, this document just may change your life.

DAY 11 BRIEFING
IDENTITY WORKSHEET

1. What are your primary jobs, hobbies, and/or courses of study? Answer based on how you actually spend your time, not on what you think will please women.

   _____
   _____
   _____
   _____
   _____

2. Which of the items you listed above best defines you?

   _____
   _____

3. What are the most interesting or adventurous aspects of the job, hobby, or course of study you selected? List each aspect, along with the ways it could affect people.

   _____
   _____
   _____
   _____

4. Now imagine you're a recruiter for the job, hobby, or course of study you selected. Using the template below, prepare an advertisement to attract people who aren't involved in the field and know little or nothing about it. Your goal is to make the job or hobby sound important and exciting.

Become a _____
                    SELECT NAME OF JOB OR HOBBY

and you can _____
                    INSERT YOUR AD LINE

Examples: Become an engineer, and you can design the mobile phone of the future. Become a guitarist, and you can tour the world playing rock shows. Become a web designer, and you can help with the images of the world's biggest corporations.

5. Now examine the ad line you wrote. Remove adjectives, adverbs, and other unnecessary hype words (such as "exciting," "biggest," "best," "most powerful"). Examine the verbs you used, and make sure they're exciting and active ("create" is better than "have"; "launch" is better than "do"). Then, using these tips, rewrite your ad line as simply, factually, and powerfully as possible in ten words or less.

_____

Example: "help with the images of the world's biggest corporations" could become "reinvent the images of corporations" or even "reinvent the images of Fortune 500 companies."

6. Rewrite your answer to question #5 in the first person (begin with the word "I").

_____

Examples: I reinvent the images of Fortune 500 companies.
I'm designing the mobile phone of the future.

7. This is your identity statement. Say it out loud until you're comfortable with it. If you feel it's uninteresting or inaccurate, rework it until it feels right—or repeat this exercise (starting with question 3) until you have an identity statement that is both truthful and interesting.

Troubleshooting

Most of the guidelines of the game are based on perceived relative status, and they change depending on how she feels your status compares to hers at any given time. So if you currently have a high-status position in society, rather than playing it up, play it down. Do exactly the opposite of what's suggested above. Keep it vague. For example, instead of telling her you're the head of a major film studio or an award-winning screenwriter, just say that you "work in movies" and let her wring the details out of you if she so desires.

MASTERING YOUR INNER GAME—A BOOK REPORT

By Thomas Scott McKenzie

A man is but the product of his thoughts.
What he thinks, he becomes.
—MAHATMA GANDHI

I am a star. I'm a star, I'm a star, I'm a star.
I am a big, bright, shining star.
—DIRK DIGGLER, BOOGIE NIGHTS

It's been proven time and time again: Confidence is attractive. Confidence earns the admiration of your coworkers, the respect of your friends, and the interest of women. In fact, it's safe to say that without confidence, all the seduction techniques known to man will not help you attract the women you desire.

But many men struggle with this most crucial of characteristics. Difficult childhoods, less-than-model looks, meager bank accounts, dead-end jobs, piece-of-shit cars, receding hairlines, underarm odor, and dating dry spells all reduce worthy men to nervous, timid mice. Even men with rock-hard abs and shiny red convertibles are sometimes unable to look women in the eye and speak with a strong voice, because a domineering mother or ex-wife damaged their self-esteem and confidence.

Mastering Your Hidden Self: A Guide to the Huna Way by Serge Kahili King offers an antidote to these confidence poisons. King teaches that we are not helpless victims vulnerable to our mind's tyranny. Instead, *we* control our minds. We control our emotions. We control our perceptions, our feelings, and our outlook. Harnessing ancient systems, King offers a concrete way to reprogram your mind so that you can stride through life with confidence, energy, and power.

INTRODUCTION TO HUNA

In addition to the widely accepted teachings of the world's great religions and philosophies, a more esoteric body of secret knowledge has been shared by initiates throughout history. Building on both the mundane and the arcane, Huna offers a system of self-improvement that cuts through the confusion of modern life.

Essentially, Huna states that you are in control of your life, your mind, and your reality. "The most fundamental idea in Huna philosophy is that we each create our own personal experience of reality, by our beliefs, interpretations, actions and reactions, thoughts and feelings," King writes.

A corollary to this is that our creative potential is unlimited. "You can create, in some form or another, anything you can conceive," King continues. This is why it's important to replace limiting beliefs based on past dating experiences with unlimited beliefs about the present and future.

Within the Huna belief system, there are seven main principles.

1. *The world is what you think it is:* The foundation of Huna, this principle asserts that you create your own personal experience of reality. "By changing your thinking, you can change your world," King writes.

2. *There are no limits:* There are no true boundaries between you and your body, you and others, or even you and God. The divisions that we generally recognize are arbitrary constraints placed by limited consciousness.

3. *Energy flows where attention goes:* When you dwell upon certain thoughts and feelings, you write the plotline for your life. Focus is the fuel for your positive or negative perceptions. So, for example, don't give some girl who ignored you the power to ruin your day by letting yourself dwell on the incident.

4. *Now is the moment of power:* At this moment, you are not hindered by any past experiences, and you are not obligated to any future duties (except paying taxes, of course). "You have the power in the present moment to change limiting beliefs and consciously plant the

seeds for a future of your choosing," King writes. "As you change your mind, you change your experience."

5. *To love is to be happy with:* People exist through love, King says, and acknowledging this allows you to exist in a state of happiness with yourself as you are now and as you will become in the future.

6. *All power comes from within:* If you want to change your reality, you can't wait for divine intervention. It's up to you to change your existence. This principle also contains King's crucial admonition that "no other person can have power over you or your destiny unless you decide to let him or her have it." For some, this means that it's time to stop blaming friends, family, work, or society for holding them back from social success and start accepting responsibility.

7. *Effectiveness is the measure of truth:* Sit in any courtroom, and you'll realize there are many versions of the truth. In an infinite universe, King writes, there is no absolute truth, only "an effective truth at an individual level of consciousness." Put simply, do whatever works for you.

THE DETRIMENTAL EFFECTS OF NEGATIVITY

To improve your inner game, it's vital that you recognize the detrimental effects of negative thoughts and energy. "Generally speaking, negative attitudes produce inner stress, which translates to physical tension and can affect organs and even cells," King writes.

The simplest way to change a negative attitude to a positive one is to be aware of bad thoughts when they appear, then consciously change them to a positive opposite. "You can do this whether or not the apparent facts of the situation seem to warrant it," King adds.

THE SUBCONSCIOUS MIND

When it comes to the subconscious, the common perception is that it lurks in the recesses of your mind, never to be known until you spend years on a therapist's couch, only to discover that you're a helpless victim of some random childhood event.

King disagrees. He explains that we can, in fact, control our subconscious. "The subconscious is not an unruly, rebellious child, nor does it ever work against your best interests . . . Whenever the *ku* [subconscious] seems to be opposing you, it is because it is following previous orders that you either gave it or allowed to remain."

A good example of how you can train your subconscious involves changing habits. Mental and physical habits are learned responses stored in your subconscious memory and released by associated stimuli. Huna teaches that the only way to eliminate a bad habit is to give your subconscious a more effective way to deal with the stimuli.

One strategy is to consider changing your speech habits. Maybe you litter your speech with brain farts and pausers. At some point in your life, perhaps these pausers allowed you extra time to choose your words. Eventually, they became a habit. Instead of accepting this bad habit or trying to quit cold turkey, Huna teaches that we must replace it. "The important point here is that there is no vacuum in the subconscious," King writes.

So instead, teach your subconscious to dump your pauser by learning to speak more slowly. Or train yourself to tap your finger against something every time you have the impulse to say "um."

Your subconscious wants to help you. It's just that sometimes the subconscious gets poor training. "Your subconscious never works against what it believes are your best interests," King writes. "Unfortunately, the assumptions on which those beliefs are based may be very faulty."

By interacting with your subconscious, King argues, you can understand your motivations and change the ones that aren't effective. He provides several strategies for interacting with your subconscious.

First of all, King suggests that you give it a name. Next, you can try one of two forms of memory search. The first is called a "treasure hunt." For this activity, simply talk to your subconscious as though you're chatting with a new pal. Name a memory of something pleasant and see what the subconscious brings back in terms of detail and vividness. Or you can ask your subconscious to return its own favorite memories. Memories you had forgotten will appear, and sensations will come flooding back.

The second form of memory search is called "trash collecting." For this activity, ask your subconscious to bring up all its worst memories. Do this enough, and you'll begin to see patterns. "The memories will follow certain themes that will provide you with clues to areas of limiting beliefs that may be hampering your development," King writes. "You may find, for instance, that a whole series of 'worst memories' in a particular session has a fear-of-rejection theme or a need-to-control theme." When it comes to women, we've all had embarrassing experiences. But if these incidents aren't properly handled in our subconscious, they can cause us to sabotage our own potential for success.

EMOTIONAL FREEDOM

One of King's main teachings is to stop being a victim to your subconscious, and instead learn to guide and instruct it.

One way to do this is by striving for what King calls emotional freedom. Stop identifying with "the emotional reactions of your subconscious," King writes. "When you say, 'I am angry,' you are identifying with the subconscious, and you may find it extremely difficult to get rid of the anger."

Instead, determine the purpose and origin of a new emotion as soon as it starts. Ask yourself, "Where did this emotion come from? Why am I feeling it right now?"

These and other questions allow you to discover the sources of your emotions. Even the act of self-examination itself can help you calm down. "The analysis itself tends to drain the emotion of its power because you are diverting the energy of the emotion to the conscious thinking process," King explains.

He also prescribes reprogramming as a technique to control your subconscious. "If you want to change the habitual thinking of the subconscious, you must consciously keep the desired pattern in the forefront of your mind until the subconscious has accepted it as a new habit." This is why affirmations, as silly as they seem sometimes, can directly improve your success with women.

THE CONSCIOUS MIND

To truly understand the conscious mind, it's necessary to understand the nature of will power. The only real ability you have on a conscious level is the power to direct your awareness and attention to a thought or experience. This is what's meant by "free will."

We can't make a woman like us, make the boss give us a raise, or make that 1974 Ford Pinto start in the morning. "What we can do, however, is to choose to decide how we are going to respond to our experience of life, what we are going to do from this moment forward and in any future moment to change either ourselves or the circumstances," King writes.

King defines determination as "the continuous, conscious directing of attention and awareness toward a given end for a purpose." And goals are achieved, he continues, "by continuously renewing the decisions or choices made to reach the given end, in spite of apparent obstacles and difficulties."

In other words, if one method does not work after repeated attempts, a determined person doesn't give up. "He tries another, and then another, until he finds one that does work, even if it means he has to change himself."

The difference, King concludes, between those with strong will and those with weak will is that the strong decide to continue, while the weak quit. It's important to remember this when the girl you've been talking to all night gives you a fake phone number, or you see a woman who just rejected your approach making out with some stranger. Failures and setbacks are fine. Deciding to quit is not.

GOALS AND PURPOSES

King makes a distinction between achieving goals and fulfilling a purpose that is key to your self-improvement journey.

The difference is that a purpose is "something that will give meaning to your whole life." A goal simply measures progress toward your purpose—like the concrete results you wrote down for your personal mission statement.

"Unlike a goal, a purpose is not something you reach but something you do," King writes. "Goals without purpose are empty of meaning, while having a purpose can give meaning to any goal."

Elsewhere in his book, King provides countless other tools for improving your mental and emotional states. By using your mind to improve your life, you can build the confidence that is an absolutely vital component to being successful with women.

As King suggests, "Look for the good in everything and, if you can't find any, figure out a way to put some in."

DAY

12

MISSION 1: Share Your Traits

Write down eight qualities you want someone to know about you. These might include individuality, humor, trustworthiness, intelligence, artistic talent, or whatever else makes you stand out.

1. _____   5. _____
2. _____   6. _____
3. _____   7. _____
4. _____   8. _____

MISSION 2: Find Your Stories

Now you know what you want to convey. But how do you convey it?

Welcome to storytelling day.

Though most women tell guys that learning to listen is important, in the early stages of an interaction, learning to speak is more important. This is because it's your job to demonstrate you're worth spending the night talking to.

Your vehicle for doing this is your past. Rather than telling women your best qualities and most charming foibles, stories allow you to show them. They also prevent you from blitzing a woman you've just met with generic questions about where she's from and what she does for work. And they provide the opportunity not just to fascinate a group of people but to inspire them to share their own stories in return.

Your tasks today will lead you toward the generation and performance of the perfect story.

You may be lucky enough to be a great storyteller already—able to hold court at countless dinner parties with the tale of that one time you had to break into a drugstore in Cairo at three in the morning to get aspirin for your girl-friend.

Or perhaps you're less loquacious, unable to think of stories on the spot or to hold anyone's attention long enough to share them. I've heard hundreds of men claim that their lives aren't interesting and they have no stories to tell. This is just another limiting belief rearing its head. It doesn't matter how small a town you live in, how little you may have traveled, how normal your family is, or how old you are, you do have interesting stories to tell. You just have to find them.

So think of the memorable moments in your life, whether they're pivotal experiences that shaped who you are as a person or just funny, trivial anecdotes that you enjoy sharing. They might be:

- ironic and embarrassing, like the time you went to relationship counseling with your girlfriend, and the therapist asked her out afterward;
- adventurous and exciting, like the time you were scuba diving, your regulator broke, and a school of barracudas swarmed around you;
- sexy and awkward, like the time the married woman sitting next to you on the plane tried to have sex with you in the lavatory;
- naive and touching, like the time your hamster died and you thought it was sleeping—for seven days;
- small and poetic, like the time you were eating a burger and suddenly realized the meaning of life;
- dangerous and heroic, like the time you saved a girl from some guy who was threatening to beat her up outside a club in Rio;
- current and confusing, about something that happened only minutes ago, like a girl you don't know coming up and asking if you'll take her sister home;
- anything you want them to be—as long as they don't evoke negative emotions in listeners or hint at negative qualities about yourself such as misanthropy, stinginess, unhappiness, prejudice, anger, or perversion.

Now think back over your childhood, family life, school, work, travel, recreation, and dating experiences, from your earliest memory to what you did last night. Extract from those experiences eight personal stories. Then give them intriguing names (like "The Magical Hamburger Incident" or "The Festering Hamster Story") and write them down in the space below:

1. _____
2. _____
3. _____
4. _____
5. _____
6. _____
7. _____
8. _____

If you're having trouble coming up with eight stories, think back on recent conversations you've had with friends and family. Try to recall any anecdotes you told that elicited excitement, intrigue, or laughter.

If you're still having trouble, imagine that you have a chance to pitch a movie about yourself to film producers. What key stories from your life would you need to include to interest them?

If you're still stuck, call a parent, sibling, or friend, and ask them to share a few favorite memories about you.

MISSION 3: Select Your Stories

Your next task is to scan the qualities you listed in Mission 1. Then look over the stories you chose for Mission 2. Mark with an asterisk each story that displays one or more of your eight qualities. Note that an ideal story does not brag or overcompensate but displays both your strengths and your vulnerabilities in an honest, humble, humorous, and engaging manner.

Of the stories you've marked, choose the two that you find most compelling and entertaining. (If you haven't marked any stories with asterisks, it's time to think of more stories—or more qualities.) List your two top stories here:

1. _____
2. _____

These are the core stories you'll work on today.

MISSION 4: Prepare Your Stories

Grab a piece of paper, pull out your journal, or open a new file on your computer.

Write out each of the two stories in their entirety. Anything goes—as long as you don't fib, because it could come back to haunt you. Here are a few tips:

■ *Have a strong beginning.* Your story needs to make a good first impression, and the best way to ensure that is to have a short, sharp, clear initial sentence. This can be a summary that flows naturally out of the conversation: "Oh, yeah, that's like the time I was forced to eat rancid shark in Iceland." It can take the form of a question that grabs the listener's interest: "Have you ever eaten rancid shark?" Or it can just be an intriguing hook: "The weirdest thing happened to me while I was in Iceland."

■ *Have a good ending.* If the story takes a surprising twist at the end, reveals the answer to a mystery posed earlier, has a non-cheesy punch line, or wraps everything up into a neat lesson, this is ideal. Either way, make sure your last sentence leaves the listener with laughter, excitement, shock, admiration, disbelief, or any strong, positive emotion. You may also want to add a question at the end, to elicit responses or similar stories from your listeners.

■ *Add intrigue.* Suspense occurs when a listener knows something is going to happen next but doesn't know either what it is or how it's going to happen. So make sure your audience is aware at all points where you're going with the story—or at least that you're going somewhere—but not how you're going to get there.

■ *Include vivid detail.* Play back the experience in your mind as you write. Close your eyes if you have to. Remember sights, sounds, smells, and feelings. The richer the detail, the more involved the listeners will become.

■ *Add humor.* Watch good stand-up comedians and you'll notice that between a set-up and a punch line, they squeeze in several additional jokes—plus a tagline after the punch line for an extra laugh. Find waypoints where you can add humor to your story. Useful devices include making fun of yourself, others, or human behavior;

comical exaggeration; references back to previous jokes; and saying the opposite of what people expect.

■ *Add value.* When illustrating your positive traits, there's a right way to brag and a wrong way. The wrong way is to declare it in a sentence: "I just bought a new car." The right way is to share it as a casual detail that helps paint a picture: "So I was driving home, and I had to unroll the window because the new car smell was suffocating me."

■ *Cut the fat.* When you're finished, reread your story. Make sure it's easy to follow and doesn't include unnecessary details and information. Mercilessly remove anything that doesn't contribute to the story. You may need to tell the story to a few people and make sure the pacing works.

■ *Cut the neediness.* Make sure that the intent of the story is to entertain, amuse, or involve other people, not to sell yourself or your accomplishments. One way to prune validation seeking is to look at every instance of the words *I* or *me,* and see how many you can remove without detracting from the story.

■ *Check the final length.* Your story should last no less than thirty seconds and no more than two minutes (that's roughly seventy-five to three hundred words on paper). If it's shorter, add more intrigue and humor. If it's longer, cut more fat.

Once you have both stories clearly written out, distill them to their major plot elements and make bullet points for each one. If, for example, you were describing *Star Wars,* the bullet points would be: Teenager living with aunt and uncle; buys two droids; discovers secret message; and so on. Unlike *Star Wars,* your stories should have only three to six bullet points.

Though you're going to practice reciting your entire story, all you need to memorize are the bullet points. This way, your delivery will seem less scripted, and you'll have more flexibility to expand and collapse the story, depending on your audience's interest level.

MISSION 5: Tell Your Stories

> *I have this theory about words. There's a thousand ways to say*
> *"Pass the salt." It could mean "Can I have some salt?"*
> *Or it could mean "I love you." It could mean*
> *"I'm very annoyed with you." Really, the list could go on and on.*
> *Words are little bombs, and they have a lot of energy inside them.*
> —CHRISTOPHER WALKEN

It's time to master the telling of your story.

The best way to captivate a listener is to be passionate. Be excited about your life, intense about your experiences, and believe in every word you say. Each time you repeat the story, it should seem like you're telling it for the first time—with all the confusion or excitement or wonder you felt when first experiencing it.

Review the vocal exercises from Day 3, then recite your two stories into your audio recorder. Make sure you speak loudly, slowly, clearly, and dynamically. To further hook listeners, stress key words and insert pauses to build suspense or humor. Experiment with emphasizing different words and pausing in unexpected places to change the rhythm of the story.

Once you're comfortable with your recitation, find a place in the middle of each story to insert an opportunity for listeners to interact. This will help keep their attention. Most interaction points will involve asking listeners if they relate to an experience, have an opinion on the experience, or can jog your memory with a fact.

For example, if you're telling a story that takes place at a Chuck E. Cheese's pizza parlor, your interaction point can simply be, "Have you ever been there? Okay, so you know what I'm talking about." If it takes place in an airport, you can ask: "It was kind of like that movie where Tom Hanks plays the guy stuck in an airport. What was it called?"

If you want to take your performance to the next level, practice casually pausing at the climax of the story to build suspense. You can take a sip of your drink, put a mint in your mouth, or, if you smoke, light a cigarette.

After you've made a successful recording of your stories, go back to the piece of paper or computer file where you originally wrote them and update them. Add any interaction points, pauses, or other embellishments you came up with while working on your delivery.

MISSION 6: Perform Your Stories

You've reached the final step in preparing your stories.

Stand in front of a mirror or set up a video camera to film yourself.

Watch yourself recite the story.

The key to a good performance is being expressive. Facial animation, eye movements, hand gestures, body language, and energy level can all tell a story as powerfully as the words themselves.

Experiment with accentuating different thoughts and emotions in the story with specific movements. Try changing your gestures or tone of voice when you're quoting other people. And feel free to use any props within arm's reach—a cell phone, a straw, or another person.

However, be careful not to overdo it. The smaller and more subtle your gestures and affectations are, the more credible they'll be. Don't get overly hyper or spastic, and make sure you have the attention and interest of the group at all times, allowing them to contribute when they want to. Don't blitz them with unrelated stories back to back; that could push you over the line from conversational expert to conversational terrorist.

There's one final element of the performance that you can't practice in front of a mirror: the unpredictable. As anyone who's been onstage will tell you, no matter how much preparation you've done, everything changes once the spotlight is shining on you.

So when you're talking to a group, don't worry about getting every gesture and phrase right. Just make sure you hit the bullet points. And if people ask questions, interrupt you, or suddenly start telling their own related story, don't get flustered. This is a good thing: It means they're paying attention.

If the conversation veers off course, don't insist on finishing your story unless your listeners ask what happened next. You can always keep the conclusion on tap for later in the evening to fill in an awkward conversational lull. Don't forget that the purpose of the story is not to get to the end, but to further display your magnetic personality.

On the other hand, don't tolerate rude behavior. Comedians deal with hecklers all the time. Have a few lines on tap for troubleshooting. A friend of mine, for example, jokes, "The show's over here," whenever someone gets distracted.

MISSION 7: Share Your Stories

Use your two stories—with interaction points—at least twice in conversation today. You don't have to tell the same person both stories; just make sure you use each story at least twice over the course of the day.

It doesn't matter whether you tell them to a woman you're interested in, a coworker, a friend, a parent, a stranger, a sibling, or a telemarketer, as long as you tell them.

Feel free to improvise. As you tell the stories, you may insert new details, jokes, and interaction points in the moment. After each successful recitation, return to your master story file and note anything you want to add, change, or remove to improve the telling.

If either of the stories doesn't hold your listeners' attention, replace it with another story from your list. If the new one doesn't work either, ask someone who was there at the time to give you feedback on your delivery or tell you his or her version of the events. If both stories get great reactions, start crafting new ones.

And congratulate yourself. Storytelling is one of civilization's oldest arts, and you're now officially part of that tradition.

DAY
13

MISSION 1: Get a Date Book

Turn to your Day 13 Briefing. Tear out the calendar page or make a photocopy. If you don't want to remove the page and don't have access to a photocopier, there's a copy available for you to print at www.stylelife.com/challenge.

MISSION 2: Promote Literacy

Head to a bookstore, preferably one with a café or sitting area. Bring the Stylelife calendar page, something to write with, and your journal, if you've been keeping one.

Get comfortable. You're going to perform the rest of today's tasks at the bookstore.

MISSION 3: Borrow Some Culture

Pick up a copy of a local events guide. This can be a free weekly newspaper, a magazine-style going-out guide, or a daily paper. You may also want to grab a local Zagat guide to restaurants or nightlife, or even a travel guidebook that includes local attractions. Since you won't be leaving the bookstore with these, you don't need to pay for them.

MISSION 4: Become Cosmopolitan

Pick up the current issue of *Cosmopolitan* magazine.

MISSION 5: Plan Your Nights

Sit somewhere comfortable in the store, like the café. Whip out your Stylelife calendar, and look through the listings, reviews, and recommendations in the paper or reference material you picked up.

Select an interesting event, restaurant, concert, gallery opening, reading, flea market, or other activity for each day of the week. Write the information for each event in the left-hand column of the calendar. The simpler and cheaper the activity, the better. Free is good too. Make sure it's something you are able to attend—not a concert that's sold out or a restaurant that's out of your price range.

In the larger column on the right side of the calendar, write one or two compelling sentences convincing someone why he or she should go to each event.

MISSION 6: Is That What They Really Think?

Read the issue of *Cosmopolitan* front to back.

First, note that women are just as desperate as men to get a date, keep a mate, and avoid rejection. Next, find an interesting topic of conversation inspired by an article, column, letter, or advertisement.

Once you choose a topic, comment on it to a woman seated nearby or wandering past. (If she's walking, speak to her while she's still coming toward you—if you see her back, you're generally too late.) Show her the story in the magazine, and tell her your reaction to it or ask a question about female behavior based on it.

If she responds favorably, then congratulate yourself. You've just generated your own spontaneous routine. If she doesn't, keep reading and find another interesting topic. Repeat with a different woman.

If she happens to ask why you have a copy of *Cosmopolitan,* tell her the truth: Someone recommended reading it to learn more about women.

There's no need to continue the conversation afterward. But if she's enjoying the interaction, feel free to proceed by using one of your openers, personal stories, or disqualifiers. Your mission is complete once you've talked about the magazine with three different women.

When you return home, add any *Cosmopolitan* routine you successfully used to the stories list you started yesterday.

DAY 13 BRIEFING

Sunday	
Monday	
Tuesday	
Wednesday	
Thursday	
Friday	
Saturday	

DAY

MISSION 1: Demonstrate Value

When you learned openers, one of the keys was to give a time constraint by saying you're going to leave shortly.

Your goal today is to be so cool and interesting that she doesn't want you to leave. The quickest way to reach this goal—the hook point—is to demonstrate value. After all, she has the possibility of meeting any number of guys that day. Why you?

For some women, just your having the confidence to approach might be enough to make you stand out from other men. For others, your sense of humor or your particular look may distinguish you. Perhaps you remind her of her first boyfriend, have a don't-give-a-shit attitude, or possess some other quality that excites her. But sometimes—especially with women who have a lot of options—you're going to have to do something a little extra.

One of the best and most efficient ways to make an impression is to teach her something about herself.

Your task is to turn to your Day 14 Briefing, read the note about using scripted material, then study the following routine and learn to give value to those you meet instead of taking value. Remember that, as with everything you've learned, there's no power in the routine itself. Your goal is simply to make her day or night better and more interesting than it was before she met you.

Once you've memorized the routine, move on to today's field assignment.

MISSION 2: Take Her Hand

Today you're going to add the rings routine to your growing repertoire.

Go any place where people gather—café, bar, park, museum, department store—and start a conversation using one of your new openers.

Afterward, as you learned on Day 11, pretend that you're about to leave. Then spontaneously notice the ring on her finger (or the lack thereof) and transition into the routine. Until you reach the hook point, and you're sure she's intrigued, continue to pretend as if you're about to leave at any moment.

If she's with friends, don't forget to include them in the conversation.

Her reaction to the rings routine doesn't matter. Whether she's fascinated or bored, you're doing this only to practice demonstrating value. Remember, these routines work best when performed in the spirit of curiosity and fun, not as a way to make an impression or get her to like you. As long as you're saying it and she's still standing there, you're completing the mission.

Feel free to continue the interaction if it's going well. If you don't know what to do after this routine, it's okay to politely make your exit. In the following week, you'll be given tools to continue the conversation, amplify the connection, and exchange numbers.

After you have practiced the rings routine on three separate women, your field mission for today is complete.

MISSION 3: What's Darwin Got to Do with It?

All this may seem like a lot of work.

After all, you're an amazing, unique individual. You've got your own life and family and friends. You're going places in the world. Why should you have to bend over backward just to meet the standards of some woman you barely even know?

The answer, my friend, is evolution.

Ultimately, whether you like it or not, in our species—and most species—men typically compete for women, and women choose men.

In your Day 14 Briefing, you'll find a book report by Stylelife coach Thomas Scott McKenzie on Matt Ridley's *The Red Queen*. Your assignment is to read the report and discover the evolutionary logic behind many of the things you've been doing this month. Keep in mind that cultural forces are at play as well in our behavior—though, of course, an evolutionary biologist would say that those forces are also shaped by natural selection.

DAY 14 BRIEFING
A NOTE ON THE MATERIAL INCLUDED IN THIS BOOK

One day I turned on the television and saw an episode of *CSI: Miami*. The plot was about a group of pickup artists using material that came word-for-word from my book *The Game*. It was the top-rated show in its time slot, reaching some fifty million viewers in fifty-five countries. Nonetheless, pickup artists around the world continued to use this exact same material, and I never heard a report of a single one getting caught because of the show.

So never underestimate people's capacity to forget the exact words they hear and where they came from

But, for argument's sake, let's imagine a worst-case scenario: You run an opener, and the woman knows it came straight from the pages of this book.

No problem.

All you need is a contingency plan. And the premise of the plan is that you now both have something in common. You've both read the same book. So just drop the opener and exclaim, "No way. You know about the book. What do you think of it? I actually decided to test it out today—and on my first approach, I get busted!"

If the goal of the opener is to start a conversation, you're now officially in one, talking about one of the most interesting topics in the world: relationships.

There is no reason to fear any outcome you can imagine. Because if you can imagine it, you can prepare a contingency plan in case it happens.

In the bigger picture, remember that the language and wording don't matter nearly as much as the intent behind them. The shady friend opener works not because it's the shady friend opener but because it's a way to start an engaging conversation with a group of people without hitting on anyone. As long as you can always do that, you've got nothing to worry about if these techniques ever become widespread.

Knowledge won't change the fundamentals of how men and women are attracted to each other. And attraction, as you're about to read, has operated on the same principles since the dawn of man.

With that in mind, the following routine is just one example of demonstrating value. Feel free to study or use anything else during the Challenge that serves the same purpose—whether it be non-cheesy magic that doesn't involve cards, visualization games like the cube, personality assessment skills like handwriting analysis, or anything else that serves the end goal of being excellent.

THE RINGS ROUTINE

QUICK-START GUIDE

- Thumb = Poseidon, representing individuality, independence, and iconoclasm
- Index = Zeus, representing dominance, power, and energy
- Middle = Dionysus, representing irreverence, rebelliousness, and decadence
- Ring = Aphrodite, representing love, romance, and connection
- Pinky = Ares, representing conflict, assertiveness, and competitiveness
- No Ring = Hermes, representing friendliness, helpfulness, and adventurousness

PERFORMANCE SCRIPT

YOU: I have to ask before I run: Why did you choose to wear that ring on that particular finger?

HER: No particular reason.

YOU: Interesting. Do you always wear rings on that same finger?

HER: I guess. Most of the time.

YOU: The reason I'm asking is because I have a friend who's a spiritual type, and she just taught me that the finger you choose to wear your rings on actually says something about your personality. I don't know if I totally believe it, but she nailed my personality pretty accurately.

If she's not wearing any rings, use this alternative: "I have to ask before I run: I notice you're not wearing any rings. Do you usually wear rings?" Then continue with the paragraph above, but say, "She just taught me that wearing rings on certain fingers, or making the choice not to wear rings, actually says something about your personality."

> YOU: In ancient Greek culture, each one of the mounds at the top of the palm was represented by a different god. And people back then would wear a ring on the associated finger to honor that particular god.

Now go through her different fingers one by one. If it seems like you have time, save the finger her ring is on for last to build intrigue.

> YOU: For example, the thumb represents Poseidon, the god of the sea. And he was very independent. He was the only god who didn't live on Mount Olympus. And the thumb kind of stands apart from the other fingers. So people with thumb rings are generally independent thinkers who tend to do their own thing. They don't follow trends; they like to set their own.
>
> The index finger is represented by Zeus, the king of the gods. And it represents power and dominance. Just like when parents scold children, they always wave the index finger. So people with a ring on this finger generally have an inclination to take charge.

If she says that the finger her ring is on doesn't fit her personality, tell her that people sometimes choose those fingers because they're subconsciously working on cultivating that particular attribute or because they're attracted to people with that attribute.

> YOU: The middle finger is represented by Dionysus, the god of wine and partying. He was a very irreverent god. And he liked to free people from their inhibitions. So if you have a ring there, it means you tend to do whatever you want without depending too much on what others think. You can be an instigator sometimes. So it kind of makes sense that it's the finger people use to swear.
>
> Your ring finger is, of course, represented by Aphrodite. She was the goddess of love, and that's supposedly why we wear wedding rings on that finger. Interestingly, it's the only finger that has a vein

that goes straight to the heart without branching off. So when someone puts a ring on that finger, they're actually making a direct connection with your heart.

If she's comfortable enough with you to allow light touching, you can hold
up her hand or touch her fingers as you do this. If she's shown more interest,
you can even trace the line of her vein from her finger up her arm.

YOU: The pinky is represented by Ares, the god of war. That's why you
see mobsters wearing pinky rings. It represents conflict. When people put the ring on themselves, back then it meant they were in conflict with themselves or had some inner turmoil. If it was given as a
gift, that often meant there was an element of conflict or competitiveness with the giver beneath the surface.

If she's not wearing any rings, add the following:

YOU: People who didn't wear rings were aligned with Hermes, who was
the messenger of the gods. He represented exotic travel and wealth,
and loved the best of everything. But he wasn't greedy. He was
known for his giving nature, and was the most helpful of the gods.
He was also the most adventurous. So people with no rings tend to
be open minded, and enjoy travel and being around others.

THE EVOLUTION OF SEXUAL PREFERENCE—A BOOK REPORT

By Thomas Scott McKenzie

In the book report on *Mastering Your Hidden Self*, we learned that everyone is
shaped by his or her environment, experiences, beliefs, and expectations. In
The Red Queen: Sex and the Evolution of Human Nature by Matt Ridley, we
learn that we're also shaped by millions of years of evolution.

Understanding the evolutionary nature of attraction and mating, as well as
the correlations in the animal kingdom, is essential in understanding our own
sexual strategies.

According to Ridley, the most powerful tool we've evolved when it comes to meeting women is our mind: "Most evolutionary anthropologists now believe that big brains contributed to reproductive success either by enabling men to outwit and outscheme other men . . . or because big brains were originally used to court and seduce members of the other sex," he writes.

WHY MEN PREFER BEAUTIFUL WOMEN

Many men tend to think that women in their particular city or country are different and require a unique seduction strategy. Not only is this not true today, according to the experiences of tens of thousands of students, but it's not true evolutionarily as well. Wherever you go, the game largely remains the same.

"Until very recently the life of a European was essentially the same as that of an African," Ridley writes. He explains that both groups hunted meat and gathered plants, made tools from the same materials, utilized complex languages, and raised children in similar manners. Advances such as metalworking, agriculture, and written language, he continues, "arrived less than three hundred generations ago, far too recently to have left much imprint . . . There is, therefore, such a thing as universal human nature, common to all peoples."

He cites a study involving more than a thousand subjects in thirty-seven countries. The statistical evidence revealed that "men pay more attention to youth and beauty, women to wealth and status."

These universal principles of selection exist not because human beings around the world are shallow but because they want to bear as many offspring as possible and have their offspring survive. Thus, according to Ridley, the male obsession with beautiful women is not so much about form as it is about function: "Prettiness is an indicator of youth and health, which are indicators of fertility."

Even the saying that gentlemen prefer blondes, Ridley claims, goes back to a correlation between blondeness and youth.

WHY WOMEN PREFER HIGH-STATUS MEN

Men have it easier than women in the looks department. "In a survey of 200 tribal societies, two scientists confirmed that the handsomeness of a man depends on his skills and prowess rather than his appearance," Ridley writes.

Study after study has shown that women are attracted to personality, dominance, and status. "In a monogamous society, a woman often chooses a mate long before he has had a chance to become a 'chief,' and she must look for clues to his future potential rather than rely only on past achievements," Ridley writes. "Poise, self-assurance, optimism, efficiency, perseverance, courage, decisiveness, intelligence, ambition—these are the things that cause men to rise to the top of their professions. And not coincidentally, these are the things women find attractive."

In other words, if you exhibit the right traits for success, some women will take a chance on you even if you're currently unemployed.

One of those traits is body language. Ridley describes an experiment where scientists recorded an actor doing two fake interviews. "In one, he sat meekly in a chair near the door, with his head bowed, nodding at the interviewer, while in the other he was relaxed, leaning back and gesturing confidently," he writes. "When shown the videos, women found the more dominant actor more desirable as a date and more sexually attractive."

WHY POPULARITY MATTERS

Ridley points out that peacocks are among the few birds to gather together in groups for sexual selection. Scientists call this gathering a lek. "The characteristic of the lek is that one or a few males, usually those that display near its center, achieve the most matings. But the central position of a successful male is not the cause of his success so much as the consequence: Other males gather around him."

Elsewhere in the chapter, Ridley writes that in experiments with guppy fish, when a female is allowed to see two males—one courting a female, the other not—she later prefers the male who was with the female, even if the courted female is no longer present.

Female competitiveness and social proof—the idea that individuals emulate what they see others in their peer group doing—seem to be effective, even in the animal kingdom.

WHY WOMEN GET TO CHOOSE

The instinctual goal for female animals is to find a mate with the genetic makeup necessary to be a good provider or a good father. Male animals, on the other hand, have a goal of locating as many wives and mothers as possible.

The reason for these disparate goals is *investment*. The gender that invests the most in children (by carrying a fetus for months, for instance) is the one that has the least to gain from extra mating. On the other hand, the gender that invests the least in children has the most extra time to spend searching for additional mates.

These different goals lend a scientific authority to something every man who's entered a singles club immediately learns: Males compete for the attention of females.

Ridley continues, "The male's goal is seduction: He is trying to manipulate the female into falling for his charms, to get inside her head and steer her mind his way. The evolutionary pressure is on him to perfect displays that make her well disposed toward him and sexually aroused so that he can be certain of mating."

Ridley examines the mating habits that revolve around peacock tails, deer antlers, swallow tailfeathers, and the colors of butterflies and guppies. The bottom line is that "females choose; their choosiness is inherited; they prefer exaggerated ornaments; exaggerated ornaments are a burden to males. That much is now uncontroversial."

For many women, high heels, push-up bras, tight clothing, and waxed body hair are just part of being fashionable and attractive. If you want to be successful with women, you have to be willing to carry a similar burden. It may feel unnatural or uncomfortable sometimes, but wearing clothes that distinguish you from the herd conveys confidence, leadership and individuality (as long as the clothes aren't wearing you). As Ridley puts it, "There is no preference for the average."

WHY MEN PURSUE CASUAL SEX MORE THAN WOMEN

Ridley argues that our different attitudes toward sex are determined by consequences. Historically speaking, casual sex for a man was a fairly low-risk activity with a huge potential payoff: "a cheap addition of an extra child to his genetic legacy," as Ridley puts it. "Men who seized such opportunities certainly left behind more descendants than men who did not. Therefore, since we are by definition descended from prolific ancestors rather than barren ones, it is a fair bet that modern men possess a streak of sexual opportunism."

Conversely, women faced massive risks when it came to casual sex. In the generations before reliable birth control, a married woman could be left with a pregnancy and potential revenge from her husband. If she was unmarried, then she could be doomed to a life of spinsterhood. "These enormous risks were offset by no great reward. Her chances of conceiving were just as great if she remained faithful to one partner, and her chances of losing the child without a husband's help were greater. Therefore, women who accepted casual sex left fewer rather than more descendants, and modern women are likely to be equipped with suspicion of casual sex."

Ridley points to interesting studies that further support his theories on promiscuity, citing research estimating that 75 percent of gay men in San Francisco have had more than one hundred partners (25 percent have had more than one thousand), while in contrast most lesbians have had fewer than ten partners in their lifetime.

WHY MEN AND WOMEN CHEAT

One interesting conclusion suggested by Ridley's book is that human beings are naturally monogamous, but they're also naturally adulterous.

Though Ridley says that women are less inclined toward casual sex, that doesn't mean they aren't promiscuous. But their promiscuity often has a purpose. For examples, Ridley looks to the animal kingdom—specifically to the phenomenon of adultery among colonial birds.

Like many human beings, female colonial birds divide men into two different categories: lovers and providers. "When a female mates with an attractive male, he works less hard and she works harder at bringing up the young," Ridley writes. "It is as if he feels that he has done her a favor by providing superior genes and therefore expects her to repay him with harder work around the nest. This, of course, increases her incentive to find a mediocre but hardworking husband and cuckold him by having an affair with a superstud next door."

Ridley closes his discussion of this topic with a crude summary of the hunter-gatherer rules that he claims still exist deep in the minds of women: "It began with a woman who married the best unmarried hunter in the tribe and had an affair with the best married hunter, thus ensuring her children a rich supply of meat. It continues with a rich tycoon's wife bearing a baby that grows up to resemble her beefy bodyguard. Men are to be exploited as providers of parental care, wealth, and genes."

WHY MEN LIKE PORN MORE THAN WOMEN

One of Ridley's more interesting asides concerns studies on male and female arousal.

Men are generally aroused by visual images; hence the success of pornography and *Maxim*. But what is the equivalent of pornography for women? His answer: romance novels, which have hardly varied for decades.

What turns women on in romance novels, however, isn't their descriptions of dashing men or lurid sex. Sex in romance novels, he explains, "is described mainly through the heroine's emotional reaction to what is done to her—particularly the tactile things—and not to any detailed description of the man's body."

The point is that women are aroused through emotional reactions, and the key to these are words and touch. So to become a master seducer, you must become a master of language and the female body.

According to another study of heterosexual men and women, men are more aroused by group sex, while women are more aroused by heterosexual couples. Yet both heterosexual women and men are aroused by lesbian scenes, while neither is aroused by male homosexual scenes. So if you're one of those men who thinks that sending a woman a close up naked picture of his abs or his genitalia is going to turn her on, think again.

WHY THE STYLELIFE CHALLENGE?

The Red Queen explains how our mating choices are the result of evolutionary and biological pressures exerted over thousands of years, providing scientific proof for the social improvement strategies discussed, such as dressing sharp, demonstrating value, raising social status, displaying personality, and projecting confidence.

Even the idea that your friends will give you a hard time as you improve is cited in this book as a normal evolutionary result of your success: Males want to destroy competitors, even the ones they secretly want to emulate.

And, finally, if you want to improve your confidence, Ridley says you're doing the right thing by going out and working to craft the perfect approach.

"We measure our own relative desirability from others' reactions to us," he writes. "Repeated rejection causes us to lower our sights; an unbroken string of successful seductions encourages us to aim a little higher."

MIDPOINT
COACHING SESSION

Pull up a seat and let's talk about life.

Here's the secret of success: What you get out of something is equal to what you put into it.

Why am I telling you this now?

Well, as a wise website once told me, "People don't fail. They just stop trying."

The midway point is a dangerous time in most regimens, and I want to make sure you're not going to bail out on the brink of a breakthrough.

Maybe you're doing just fine and anxious to press forward. But if you're anything like the majority of past Challengers, you're beating yourself up mentally before and during the field assignments.

Over what? Why are you giving these strangers power over you?

They are walking sources of feedback—there to give you insight about yourself and teach you how to do better next time. They're not even judging you nearly as much as you're judging yourself over this.

If I'd gotten discouraged by all the rejection letters I'd received (not to mention by the incoherent prose of my first stories), I wouldn't be writing today.

But I learned from every paragraph, every mistake, every critique, every success.

So guess what?

This is a challenge. That means it's going to be challenging.

Not difficult, just challenging—to the bad habits that never worked for you in the first place.

You've been offered an olive branch to fix yourself.

Are you going to take it and run with it, or are you going to just stand there and hit yourself over the head with it?

Every single person I know who's dazzlingly successful with women worked hard to get where he is. Whether he admits it now or not, he's overcome amazing obstacles—the biggest of which has been himself.

All the frustrations (as well as the highs) you're experiencing as you complete these assignments, we've all experienced. And what separates the ones who succeed from the ones who don't is their commitment to themselves, to the game, and to getting in the field and playing their best.

One of the most frustrating things about the game is that it requires effort. No matter how much status you may have at work or in school, you don't have more status than that jaw-dropping woman who's dressed to kill and turning every head as she glides through the club. No one does. Not the rock star. Not the billionaire. She can have her pick of the litter. And she can pick you. But it's going to take commitment.

Every time you don't approach, every time you don't try, every time you give up on something, every time you just go through the motions, every time you talk yourself out of a new or uncomfortable experience, the only person who loses is you.

To quote Wayne Gretzky on hockey: "You miss one hundred percent of the shots you never take."

It's time to take that shot.

DAY

15

MISSION 1: Cold Reading

Today you're going to learn one of the quickest ways to distinguish yourself from other men. Using this technique, you can very quickly enter the minds of strangers and tell them things even their best friends may not know.

Your assignment: Turn to your Day 15 Briefing and read the primer on cold reading.

MISSION 2: See a Psychic (Optional)

Your mission: Go to a psychic and get a reading.

If you have a portable audio recorder, ask to record the session.

The only reason this is optional is because it costs money, typically from five to forty dollars—don't pay more. However, I strongly recommend it for all Challengers.

Most communities have a few storefronts, New Age bookstores, and street fairs where psychic readers can be found. If you don't know where to find a local palm reader, tarot reader, or other fortune-teller, check the guide to local events you read on bookstore day, or go to Google Maps (http://maps.google .com) and search "psychic mediums." If you still can't find one, as a last resort call the American Association of Professional Psychics at 1-800-815-8117 (or, internationally 1-561-207-2391) and buy a ten-minute reading by phone.

Warning: Though most psychics are trustworthy, some are not. So don't give out financial, credit card, or personal identifying information. In addition, you shouldn't pay more than the initially quoted fee; if they ask for money after the reading to warn you of an impending event, don't fall for it. Thank them for their time and leave.

MISSION 3: Rate Your Reading

The following task is for all Challengers, whether or not you've gone to a psychic. (If you haven't, for reasons of money or time, go to www.stylelife.com/challenge. Input the date, time, and location of your birth, and get your astrological chart. Read the information as if you're getting your fortune told.)

Spend a few minutes analyzing the information you received during your psychic session, based on the cold-reading article you read today. Ask yourself the following questions:

- Did you feel the reading was good or bad? Why?
- Did you feel the reader was performing a generic routine or genuinely connecting with you? Why?
- Did you feel the reader understood you less or more than some of your friends? Why?
- Do you believe the reader had extra sensory powers? Why or why not?
- Would you visit the reader again? Why or why not?

Take a moment to reflect on these answers and what they tell you about the characteristics of a good or bad cold reading. If there were any lines or phrases from the psychic reading that particularly resonated with you, write them down in the space below:

_____

_____

_____

Consider using these lines and phrases when performing your own cold readings.

DAY 15 BRIEFING
THE SECRET ART OF COLD READING

By Neil Strauss, Don Diego Garcia,
and Thomas Scott McKenzie

Most Challengers fit a certain personality profile, known as the Explorer, and chances are that you're one of them. If so, the following analysis may apply to you:

Explorers acknowledge that they have a few personality flaws, but they're usually able to compensate for them with their ability to keep up appearances. This is because, beneath the surface, they have an incredible amount of personal potential just waiting to be tapped. They try to seek variety in their encounters and feel like a caged tiger when too many rules are forced on them.

Explorers have a tendency to be a little hard on themselves sometimes but find solace in positive encouragement. At the same time, they take pride in their independence and don't just blindly accept the opinions of others. That doesn't mean, however, that they don't have a part of them that wants—and perhaps even needs—to be liked by those around them.

As Explorers grow a little older, they develop more secrets. And though they continue to work on themselves and make progress, they sometimes look back and wonder if they've made all the right decisions in life. A few of their dreams remain achievable in the near future, while a couple of others are a bit fanciful.

If you found yourself nodding and agreeing at any point, you have just discovered the power of cold reading. In short, the art of cold reading is making a truism sound like a revelation. *Cold* refers to the fact that the person knows nothing about you. And *reading* refers to when your experiences, thoughts, desires, and future events are told to you as though they were lifted from the pages of a book.

And they were. The script above is based on a classic reading, which has been passed on through generations of fortune-tellers.

History

In 1948, psychologist B. R. Forer gave a personality test to his students. Regardless of how they answered, Forer gave everyone the exact same personality profile afterward. He then asked the students to evaluate the accuracy of the profile. A score of 5 meant that the recipient felt the profile was excellent.

The class average turned out to be 4.26. So all these unique, individual human beings were told the exact same thing, yet they felt the words fit them almost entirely accurately. The conclusion: People tend to accept vague and general personality descriptions as being completely relevant to themselves. Furthermore, people usually accept claims about themselves in proportion to their desire that the claims be accurate.

These principles help explain why palm readers make a living, why people devour horoscopes in the paper every day, and why psychic hotlines exist.

Cold Reading and Attraction

If everyone's favorite subject is himself or herself, imagine the excitement they must feel when they meet a stranger who seems to know them almost as well as they know themselves.

So it's no surprise that cold reading occupies a central place in the art of attraction. Here are just a few of its uses:

- *The cold-reading opener:* Making an intelligent observation or sharing an intuition about a woman can be an effective way to spark her curiosity, and prompt her to stop and talk to you. Phrases like "I have an intuition that . . . ," "Something tells me that . . . ," or "I just noticed that . . ." are good ways to preface your observation.
- *The cold-reading hook:* Sometimes it's necessary in an interaction to demonstrate that you stand out from the tools who usually come on to her. If you say something incredibly insightful and perceptive about her early in the conversation, she may begin to realize that she's met someone rare and special.
- *The cold reading amplifier:* Yesterday you learned the rings routine, one of many tests, games, and demos at your disposal for showing higher value. A knowledge of cold reading is essential to turn these

demonstrations from mildly amusing ways of killing time to emotionally connecting experiences.

Ethics

Keep it positive.

Never predict anything negative in the future or anything that will cause harm. When pointing out a personality flaw, even if it's accurate, present it in a reassuring way.

Don't tell her, "You're really insecure." Instead, say, "You may not be the most confident person in the room, but deep down you know your own value."

Never use cold-reading scripts in a callous, manipulative way—especially as a scam to con women into believing that they share an intense, metaphysical connection with you. Instead, use cold reading as a legitimate conversation starter, connection builder, or way to demonstrate your unique knowledge of human behavior.

Finally, cold reading is a secret art that's traditionally passed from teacher to student. Do not use the term *cold reading* with the women and groups you approach, and do not share this information.

Vehicles, Props, and Systems

A cold reading can consist of just a line or two of insight about the person you're talking to, or it can fuel a half-hour-long demonstration of value.

A prop, classification system, or something specific to anchor your cold reading will give you the credibility, authority, and pretext you need to make your reading as long as you want. In general, save readings that last more than a few minutes for quiet environments and one-on-one moments after the hook point.

Any number of props exist to give authority to cold readings. These range from well-known tools like tarot cards, rune stones, and the book of I Ching to more esoteric forms of divination like scrying (crystals) and cubomancy (dice). If you don't want to carry around these items, there are many systems that require nothing but knowledge, including palm reading, numerology, astrology, and the rings routine you learned yesterday.

When meeting women in bars and clubs, you can also springboard into cold reading based on something that's normally part of the interaction or environment. For example, after shaking a woman's hand, you might begin cold reading based on the strength and grip of her handshake. You can even assess her personality based on the cocktail she's drinking, the position of the straw in her glass, or the way she's worn down the tip of her lipstick.

Psychological personality profiles and their accompanying jargon are one of the best ways to give your reading an increased air of authority and expertise. One such system is the social-styles model, which places people into one of four categories depending on their assertiveness and responsiveness. Here are the broad strokes of how it works:

To evaluate her assertiveness, ask if she's the kind of person who asks her friends what they want to do when they go out or tells them what the plan is. To figure out her responsiveness, ask if she's the kind of person who tells people when she's upset or keeps it to herself.

Based on her answers, you can create a cold reading based on the social-styles personality type she falls into:

- If she makes plans by asking for opinions and keeps her emotions to herself, then she's an *analytical*.
- If she makes plans by telling her friends what she's doing and keeps her emotions to herself, she's a *driver*.
- If she makes plans by asking and shares her emotions, she's an *amiable*.
- If she makes plans by telling and shares her emotions, she's an *expressive*.

Each of these personality types is associated with further behavioral traits, which can be researched online. Other systems worth looking into include the Enneagram and the Myers-Briggs Type Indicator.

The Cold Reading Code

Remember the Golden Rule—always tell the subject
what he/she wants to hear!
—RAY HYMAN, "GUIDE TO COLD READING"

There are standard guidelines and principles that fuel every cold reading. Many have been around for centuries. Here are a few of them:

CONDITIONALITY

The key principle of cold reading is to never state an impression as a definite fact. It's far safer—and more accurate—to use conditional words and general terms.

If you say, "You are shy," your listener can always respond, "No I'm not."

But if you say, "You can be shy at times," this is a lot harder to deny.

When you use conditional words, every line you say during a cold reading becomes practically irrefutable. Here are a few examples of words and phrases to preface your insights with when developing your own cold-reading material: *a part of you, at times, every now and then, somewhat, generally, now and again, occasionally, once in a while, frequently, tendency,* and *sometimes.*

If you have some idea of your partner's disposition or the universality of your statement, you can use words and phrases with a narrower range of interpretation—like *usually, often, rarely, seldom, many, hardly, normally, regularly,* and *almost never.*

Unless you know for certain that your information is accurate, avoid absolute words and phrases such as *always, completely, every, all the time, none of the time, entirely,* and *never.*

FALSE SPECIFICITY

Though you want to avoid absolutes, this doesn't mean you can't punch up your reading with phrases that imply specificity.

One way to accomplish this is to use transition words like *because,* which imply causality even when a link doesn't exist.

Another way to make your reading sound specific is to affirm the listener's individuality by showing how her traits contrast with the norm. This can be accomplished by using a sentence structure like: "Though many people _____, you tend to _____."

CONFIDENCE

Act as if you're certain that everything you say is true. Even when you make a mistake or claim something that's not entirely accurate, if you say it with authority, most people will still believe it. On the other hand, doubt in your voice will create doubt in the listener's mind—even if what you're saying is true.

APPROVAL

People are more likely to agree with a positive statement about themselves, even when it's not true. Conversely, they're less likely to agree with a negative statement, even if it's accurate.

Welding these two principles together helps create one of the most powerful and beneficial things you can do when talking to a woman: to recast what she or others believe to be her negative traits into more positive ones.

If she's shy, for example, tell her, "Though some people think of you as shy, the truth is that you just take a while to get comfortable around new people."

Or if you're talking to a beautiful woman who's a little icy, you can tell her, "Some people think you're stuck up, but that's not true. You're just uncomfortable sometimes, and because of the way you look, people mistake your shyness for meanness."

AFFIRMATION

This is a simple technique that will make a big difference in a woman's judgment of your accuracy. Whenever you can, pause and get her either to agree explicitly with what you're saying or just respond with words like *yes* and *right*. The more yes responses she gives, the more her subconscious mind will accept you as an authority.

OPPOSITES

Some of the most powerful cold reads make a statement that contrasts two opposite qualities. For example: "At times you can be outgoing and social, while at other times you're more comfortable keeping to yourself."

This may look completely meaningless on paper, but try it out. When said with authority and understanding, it can seem incredibly insightful.

An additional technique you can use when delivering statements that contain opposites is the two-hand comparison: Lift one hand and indicate to it when you recite the first personality type, then lift and present your other hand when you describe the second type. Typically, her eyes or nose will point to the hand she has more affinity with as she considers each one.

OBSERVATION

When cold reading, it's important to be acutely aware of her reactions and facial expressions. Check to see whether her body language is affirming what you say (associative) or denying it (dissociative).

For example, without even realizing it, many people nod their head up and down while you're saying something they agree with, and shake it from side to side when they disagree. They may blush when you say one thing, and frown when you say another.

Below are examples of encouraging and discouraging cues to look for:

Associative Responses	*Dissociative Responses*
Head nodding up and down	Head shaking side to side
Eyebrows raising	Eyebrows lowering
Eyes widening	Eyes squinting
Smiling	Frowning
Body turning toward you	Body turning away from you
Animated expression	Blank expression
Arms open	Arms crossed

LISTENING

Often, people will start talking when you're cold reading them. Be quiet and listen, nodding and smiling as if these are things you already knew about them. They'll usually offer all the information you need to craft an extremely precise reading.

ADDITIONAL CLUES

When you're speaking face-to-face, you don't have to stick to scripted lines. Your eyes and ears can pick up a wealth of clues to help refine your reading. Pay focused attention to what she says, what she does, and the people with whom she chooses to surround herself.

A woman's age, ethnicity, speaking voice, style of dress, accessories, hairstyle, and jewelry are the most obvious signs of who she is. Look at her fingernails to see if they're clean or dirty, short or long, natural or painted. Notice the way she speaks, holds herself, and gestures. Does she do it with confidence or insecurity, and how does this relate to the way she looks?

Even where she's from—especially if it's a town associated with a particular university, company, or occupation—can give you extraordinary information. The more you notice, the more specific and accurate your cold reading will be.

TROUBLESHOOTING

It may just happen that as you're delivering a line, you see the woman you're talking to shaking her head negatively and folding her arms. If this happens, you need to recover. To do so, just stick to the rules: Assert your confidence and return to your conditional words. You can turn it all around through the power of just one word: *but*.

For example, if you're telling her, "You tend to be critical of yourself sometimes," and she starts to disagree, don't get flustered. Just continue speaking as if she's interrupting before hearing the complete thought: "But most of the time, you're more accepting of yourself. And this is what makes you stand out from others around you."

Be forewarned that there's one type of person you may come across who is invulnerable to cold reading. This person is what's known as a "polarity responder." Whatever you tell polarity responders about themselves, they're going to disagree. They may even get upset or angry that you claim to know anything about them.

For example, tell a polarity responder that she tends to be shy, and she'll probably respond, "I'm actually very confident." If you then simply repeat that she's confident, she'll say something like "Not always." Why? Because polarity responders just don't want to be defined. They derive their identity through their unique, uncompromising, often argumentative individuality.

Trying to cold read this kind of person is like trying to grip an eel. Eventually, you have to use a net to catch the eel. And that's exactly what you're going to do. Just smile and ask: "So you're the type of person who doesn't like to be pigeonholed?"

There is literally no way she can answer this without agreeing with you. As you watch her forehead crease and the befuddlement begin, just laugh with her, tell her you're joking, and quickly move on to another subject that doesn't involve cold reading. If her personality is really unpleasant, extricate yourself politely with your all-purpose farewell: "Nice meeting you."

Amazing Yourself

There's a next level to this talent.

Imagine walking up to a complete stranger and saying, "Out of curiosity, were you raised in a military family? . . . Yeah, I thought so . . . And you're probably the oldest sister too . . . I knew it!"

As you practice cold reading, you'll develop a strong intuition for people. Eventually, you'll find yourself going far beyond the principles described here, and you'll actually be able to guess with decent accuracy whether someone is an oldest or youngest child; what she does for work; what type of environment she was raised in; and any number of specific facts about her.

And if you happen to be wrong, you'll have the cold-reading skills to explain what led you to your conclusion in a way she'll ultimately agree with.

Sound impossible? Well, you'll learn more about how to do this when you study calibration on Day 28.

DAY

16

MISSION 1: The Missing Link

You have only one assignment today.

It's a piece that you've most likely not read about, heard about, or even imagined was part of the game. It's also subtle and will require the social and cold-reading skills you've learned thus far.

It's a piece that differentiates those who fail at the game from those who succeed—even though both may be saying the exact same thing.

It's a piece that will keep you from accidentally losing yourself in the effort to improve yourself.

It's also simple and basic. And it's one of the biggest lessons I've learned since writing *The Game*.

When I first started teaching workshops, I noticed that I could tell just by looking at a student whether or not he was going to get good reactions from women. And it had nothing to do with what he was wearing, what he looked like, or what he said. It was something intangible. A certain energy he gave off.

That's when I realized that everyone I'd met in the game, students and teachers alike, was overlooking something. But I didn't realize what that something was until months later.

Here's what happened: I had a student who'd been studying seduction for years. He's a sweet, good-hearted guy who knows every routine (even listens to them incessantly on his iPod) and goes out to meet women nearly every night. Yet he's still a virgin.

So he decided to fly to Los Angeles for a one-on-one session. He wanted me to examine him and find his Achilles' heel. I eventually found it, and it turned out to be such an epiphany that it changes the game of anyone who understands it.

Here is the key distinction:

The guy who fails at the game is the one who goes out looking for women to make him feel good about himself.

The guy who succeeds at the game is the one who goes out and makes other people feel good about themselves.

This first type of guy is someone no one wants to be around. He is needy, insecure, and reaction seeking. He will suck your energy dry in his quest for validation and approval.

This second type of guy is easy to be with. He radiates charisma and positive energy. Women enjoy his company, as do their friends, and they want him around all the time. They trust him, feel comfortable with him, and end up at his house at five o'clock in the morning wondering where all that time went.

Both guys do and say the exact same things, but they get very different reactions from women solely because of the intentions they're communicating.

Wait a minute, you may be thinking, what about disqualification? Doesn't it seem to contradict the idea of making people feel good about themselves?

Think again.

When you give a generic compliment to a woman who's often hit on, she'll usually ignore the remark—or assume you're saying it because you want to sleep with her. So instead you tease her, show her you're unaffected by her beauty, and demonstrate that you're out of her league. When she works to win *you* over, and you ultimately reward her with your approval, she will leave that night or the next morning feeling good about herself—like something special has happened and she's connected with somebody who appreciates her for who she really is.

In short, a teasing disqualification will buy you the credibility you need to sincerely compliment her later.

So today we're going to let go of our need for approval and we're going to make people feel good about themselves. Don't go to bars looking for approachable groups or cafés looking for lone women. Just go about your daily life. But three times during the day, go out of your way to make someone feel good about himself or herself.

That is your mission.

This might include telling your parent how much you appreciate them; making an awkward guest at a party feel wanted and included; telling a person who just blew a lot of money on a new outfit or haircut that it looks good; giving a homeless person eye contact, smiling, and handing over five dollars; or asking someone in a rush if they'd like to cut ahead of you in a checkout line.

Be sure to look for what people need when you do this exercise. Don't just give random compliments. And don't be concerned with whether you're raising or lowering your relative status. For example, if you see someone getting out of a new yellow Lamborghini with the dealer plates still on, instead of thinking he's an asshole and a show-off, consider that he spent a lot of money because he wants your approval. So give it to him: "Hey man, cool car. I'm jealous."

Of the three people you make feel good about themselves today, only one interaction can occur on the phone. And at least one of the people you interact with must be a stranger.

The goal is to stop worrying about what other people think of you, and start developing an instinct for what they need to feel good about themselves and their choices. You'll be amazed by the results.

After spending the weekend in L.A. and discussing these ideas, the student with the former Achilles' heel sent me the following email: "The other night, it was my twenty-sixth birthday. I was chatting up a four-set using the positive ideas we'd discussed, and one of them started groping me. Next thing you know, hardcore tongue-down makeout. First time ever!"

So get out of your head and start mastering the most intelligent and evolved emotion there is: empathy.

DAY

MISSION 1: Make No Mistake

We've covered a lot of ground in the last sixteen days.

So let's pause and make sure you're up to speed.

Welcome to review day.

Your first task is to go over the Day 17 Briefing, which covers the eleven most common mistakes guys make when opening.

Make sure you're no longer doing any of them.

MISSION 2: Check Your Core Competency

Look over the previous eight days and review each mission.

Make a list of the skills you don't feel you've mastered yet.

Your assignment is to redo each and every task you don't feel competent in.

At this point, you should be able to walk up to a woman or group, deliver an opener successfully, and transition smoothly into a value demonstration such as the rings routine. In addition, make sure you haven't slacked in your attention to your body language, speech, and appearance.

MISSION 3: Return of the Rings

Your final review mission is to go out, approach a woman or group, and perform the rings routine again.

Take your time with the delivery and incorporate the cold-reading information you learned on Day 15. Try to get a feel for the personality and self-image of the person you're talking to. Add at least one of the cold-reading scripts you heard or read on Day 15 as well as an original line based on your own assessment of the person. Notice her responses to the material.

Your mission is complete once you've successfully demonstrated the rings routine, with additional cold reading, for two different women or groups.

DAY 17 BRIEFING
THE ELEVEN COMMANDMENTS

1. Don't wait to approach her until she's alone. Even if she likes you, her friends will soon drag her away.

2. Don't stare at her for more than three seconds before approaching. Hesitate, and you'll either creep her out or psych yourself out.

3. Don't be afraid to approach just because there are men in the group. Chances are she's with family, friends, or coworkers, not a love interest.

4. Don't open a conversation by apologizing. Phrases like "Excuse me," "Pardon me," and "I'm sorry" make you sound like a beggar.

5. Don't hit on her or give her a generic compliment. Instead, start a conversation with an entertaining anecdote or question, such as asking the group to suggest names for a three-legged cat or a store that sells 1970s memorabilia. Everyone loves to give an opinion.

6. Don't buy her a drink. You shouldn't have to pay for her attention.

7. Don't touch or grab her right away. If she touches you, say, with a smile, "Hey now, hands off the merchandise."

8. Don't lean in or hover over her. Stand up straight and, if the music's too loud or she's seated, simply speak up.

9. Don't initially ask what her name is, what she does for a living, or where she's from. She's bored of talking about the same things with every new guy she meets.

10. Don't focus all your attention on her when she's with other people. If you win over her friends, you'll win her.

11. Don't be afraid to violate any of these guidelines once you understand them and why they exist.

DAY

18

MISSION 1: Sewing a Conversation

So far, you've learned a sequence of things to say and do when meeting a woman. It's now time to find out how to stitch it all together and leave her wanting more.

Your mission: Read the Day 18 Briefing on the four secrets of compelling conversation before moving on to the next assignment.

MISSION 2: Think Fast

In improvisational comedy, there's an exercise called the herald. To begin a herald, an actor asks the audience to suggest a word. As soon as an audience member offers one, the actor tells a true story from his life based on that random suggestion.

The story doesn't literally have to be about the word: It can simply be something that the word suggests or reminds him of. For example, if the audience member says "clown," the monologist can share a memory about his first time visiting the circus, about acting like a class clown in high school, or even about something that made him extremely happy or sad one day.

Afterward, the rest of the actors onstage improvise scenes based on his story; words or details in his story; or ideas his story suggests.

Your assignment is to try something similar at home: Practice spontaneously sharing true stories from your life based on one-word suggestions.

There are two ways to do this:

- Get together with a friend and take turns giving each other random words to elicit stories. It's important to start telling the story immediately, without waiting longer than ten seconds.

■ Go to www.stylelife.com/challenge. I've created a random word generator there. Base a story on the random word presented by the generator. Make sure you recite the story out loud.

Practice this exercise until you feel confident spinning a story on the spot, with a definite beginning, middle, and end, based on an arbitrary word. If you're having trouble, reread your storytelling tips from Day 12.

The goal is to develop the ability to continue a conversation effortlessly using whatever material the woman you're speaking to gives you. Every concrete word she says is a hook you can choose to pull and stretch into a story or further conversation.

MISSION 3: Multiple Thread Mission

Today's field assignment is to practice creating the open loops and multiple threads you read about in today's briefing. You're going to do this by going out and delivering an opener. This time, though, before you finish discussing the opener, start another thread.

For example, if you're delivering the shady friend opener and you want to open a new thread, all you need to do is make a spontaneous observation or excited comment. You can interject, "By the way, I have to ask, why are you wearing a ring on that particular finger?" Or you can say, "Before we get to that, you'll never believe what just happened on the way here."

Possible threads include: one of the stories you developed on Day 12, another opener, an observation about her or something in the environment, a spontaneous story inspired by something she said, or a value demonstration like the rings routine or the social styles personality assessment.

Don't worry if this feels awkward or initially makes it seem like you have attention deficit disorder. Just approach and open, and you'll find that starting another thread will come easily once you have your mind set on it.

Your assignment is complete once you've approached two groups and successfully interrupted each opener with a second thread.

Note that creating open loops during your opener isn't a necessary part of most walk-ups. However, it is important to practice doing it today.

DAY 18 BRIEFING
THE FOUR SECRETS OF COMPELLING CONVERSATION:
LOOPS, HOOKS, THREADS, AND . . .

Loops

The story collection *1001 Arabian Nights* begins with King Shahryar's discovery that his wife has been unfaithful. He kills her and declares that he can no longer trust any woman. From then on, he marries a different woman each day, spends the night with her, then executes her in the morning before she can cheat on him.

This reign of paranoid terror continues until one day he marries his match. Her name is Scheherazade. She knows that the king is planning to kill her in the morning. So on her first night with him, she starts telling a story. But just as the story reaches its climax, dawn breaks, and she stops at a cliffhanger and promises to continue the story the next night.

Curious to hear how the story ends, the king decides not to kill her that morning. And so it continues for night after night of cliffhangers, until Scheherazade has borne the king three sons, convinced him that she is faithful, and won his heart.

The principle Scheherazade employs is one known in the psychological field of neurolinguistic programming as open loops.

Simply put, creating an open loop means leaving a story or thought unfinished. This is the reason that TV series like *Lost* are so successful. Every week, these shows add more and more open loops to the plot, leaving viewers anxious for resolution on dozens of different mysteries.

When I was first learning seduction, if I wanted to get a woman's phone number or email address, I'd begin a value demonstration like the rings routine. But before I could finish it, I'd say I have to go meet friends or I'd have a friend pull me away. This way, if she wanted to hear what the rings on her fingers meant, she'd have to talk to me again.

Hooks

When talking with a woman you've just met, whenever she speaks, imagine the sentence or comment as a long horizontal string. Then imagine that there's a hook hanging down from each major word in that sentence. You have the option of pulling on any one of those hooks to start a new conversational thread.

Even a mundane line like "I've been working as a paralegal for six months" offers multiple hooks you could pull. You might tell any law-related stories you know; find out what she was doing before getting the job; ask about the office where she works; ask what exactly a paralegal does; tell her a story about one of your worst or best jobs; ask her opinion on a recent trial in the news; discuss the challenges of surviving law school; find out if she's new in town; or tell her to quit her job because you can get her a position as chief counsel in your little brother's lawn mowing business.

Even though she's hardly given you any information, she's created an endless array of hooks for you to pull on. And you can turn any of them into stories or humorous disqualifiers. To be a winning conversationalist, you generally want to grab the least obvious but most interesting hook.

Hooks also work in reverse. Instead of asking a woman questions, you can leave dangling hooks in your own conversation, selectively leaving out specific information in a way that compels her to ask you about your life. For example, if you say, "Back where I'm from, we don't do that kind of thing," she's bound to ask where you're from. Saying "Well, that may be true, unless you're in my line of work" will lead her to ask what you do. And now she seems to be chasing you.

Threads

Simply put, a thread is a single topic of conversation. For example, if you approach a group of women and deliver the shady friend opener, the thread would be the topic of jealous girlfriends. After ten minutes, though, that thread will start to wear thin. And if, in an act of desperation, you attempt to prolong the conversation by asking, "Well, what about girls who are friends with their ex-boyfriends?" it will seem as if you have nothing else to talk about.

The way to prevent this is to avoid focusing a conversation on only one topic and beating it into the ground. Instead, weave in several topics or stories at once, so that, like Scheherazade, you leave your audience captivated and wanting more. Juggling multiple open loops in a conversation will create the impression that you and the person you met have a lot to talk about.

Here's an example of creating a second thread during an opener, based on material generated during the Challenge by one of your colleagues.

> YOU: Hey, maybe you can help us settle a debate. Was there a fireman in the Village People?
>
> HER: I don't know. There was a construction worker and some leather guy.
>
> YOU: Yeah, there were five of them. And we can only figure out like, four: There's a cop, an Indian . . . By the way, really quickly, before I get to that, I just noticed your bracelet. My sister bought herself one just like it for her birthday.
>
> HER: Thanks. This was a present too, actually.
>
> YOU: Yeah, I always find it funny when people buy themselves presents for their birthdays. I mean, that doesn't count. Like one time, for my twentieth birthday . . .

Rather than talking for ten minutes about the Village People, you've started a second conversation in the middle of the opener. So when you're done talking about bracelets and presents, you can avoid an awkward silence by returning to the open loop about the Village People.

The most natural way to add a new thread to a conversation is by spontaneously noticing something new and getting more excited about it than what you were originally talking about.

This may sound artificial, but it happens all the time. Perhaps you're talking to a friend about a woman you met at the bank, but as soon as you name the bank, he interrupts to mention that he has a massive crush on a teller there. Or you're in the middle of a story, an ex-girlfriend suddenly walks past, and you pause to point her out to your friend.

Simply being aware of how to use loops, hooks, and threads can enhance your ability to make a deeper and more exciting connection with someone you've just met. They help create instant rapport, prevent potentially fatal pauses in conversation, and leave her with the impression that you two have a lot to talk about.

The Fourth Secret

Don't forget the moral of *1001 Arabian Nights*. As a species, we thrive on stories and suspense. So experiment with leaving routines unfinished, stories cut off at cliffhangers, and unresolved questions lingering in her head.

It can be as simple as saying, "There are three things I'm attracted to in other people, but I can't tell you the third thing yet because I don't know you well enough."

You can always choose to close the loop later in the conversation, during a future phone call or meeting, or never. If you leave her wanting more, you'll leave her wanting to see you again.

Finally you may be wondering about the fourth secret to compelling conversation? And I'd like to share that with you. Sometime.

DAY

19

MISSION 1: Fill Up Your Calendar

Pull out your Stylelife calendar—or print or copy a new one.

Fill in activities on the calendar—as well as selling points and reasons to go to each event—for today and the following six days. The items can be anything from restaurants to concerts to parties to roadside attractions to the psychic you went to on Day 15.

Familiarize yourself with the activities, the dates you listed them on, and the reasons for going.

MISSION 2: Seeding

You're now ready to begin the process of comfortably getting a woman's phone number.

Your first step: Turn to the Day 19 ' and read the short article on seeding.

MISSION 3: Seeding Mission

Seed three conversations today with an event from your calendar.

Two of these conversations can be with people you already know. However, at least one must be with a woman you've approached using one of your openers.

It isn't necessary to invite her to the event at the end of the conversation. The goal of today's exercise is not to get a phone number or a date (although if that does happen, great). The goal is simply to practice sprinkling a casual conversation with the seed for a future meeting.

DAY 19 BRIEFING
WHAT IS SEEDING?

Asking for a phone number can be one of the most difficult parts of an interaction with a woman you've just met. If she declines to give you her number, or instead asks for yours because she claims she doesn't give her phone number to guys, then all your previous efforts to build a connection with her have been in vain.

Even if she likes you, she may still refuse to give you her phone number the first time you ask. This is what's called an automatic or autopilot response: After experiencing repeated clumsy pickup attempts, many women have lines they use, almost by instinct, to politely decline requests for their phone number.

So what's the solution?

Don't ask for the phone number at all.

Today and tomorrow, you'll learn the two keys to exchanging phone numbers without asking.

The first key is seeding, a technique in which you mention a tempting event but do not immediately invite the woman to attend. For example, casually mention a party you're going to, talk about how cool it's going to be, and move on to other topics. Then, later in the interaction, before you're about to leave, decide to invite her to come along.

At some point in conversation with a woman I've met, I may mention my favorite local chef:

"You remember the Soup Nazi episode of *Seinfeld*? Well, this guy is the Sushi Nazi. His menu is only two words, 'Trust me,' and he just serves you what he wants. If you don't eat it in one bite, he'll stop serving you. If you dip it in soy sauce when he asks you not to, he'll cut you off. And if you dare ask for Americanized sushi, like a California roll, he'll chew you out and kick you out. But it's worth it, because the sushi literally melts in your mouth. The guy is an artist. He never smiles. He's just driven by some compulsion to make the best sushi in the world."

After I tell the story, I may even mention that I'm going there with friends on Thursday night. The obvious and expected next step would be to ask her immediately to join us. But because it's so obvious, I don't do it. I move on to other subjects and let her wonder why she wasn't invited. Only at the last minute do I turn to her and say, "Hey, you know what, you should come to the Sushi Nazi with us on Thursday."

Sure, maybe I could have invited her when I first mentioned the restaurant; maybe she would even have said yes. But the point of the game is to eliminate the word *maybe* as much as possible from interactions with women.

Seeding helps to increase the odds of her saying yes, by avoiding the kind of pressure she might feel when confronted with a sudden invitation—pressure that often triggers a negative autopilot response. Mentioning the event, and then allowing her time to think about whether she wants to go before you get around to inviting her, gives her a chance to come to an affirmative decision on her own. Especially if you've continued to display more great personality, value, and non-neediness along the way. In addition, as you learned on disqualification day, not inviting her when you first mention the event will only increase her desire to go.

Having a pretext for getting together again and a plan set in stone also drastically reduce the chances that she'll flake. Even if she's not sure about you yet, she's more likely to come along anyway, just for the experience. Tagging along with a small group of interesting people to experience the best sushi in the world or check out the funniest comedian who ever lived or go to the coolest dive bar in town is a lot more tempting than just "going for coffee" or "getting together to talk sometime," which is how many guys ask women out. And compared to an actual date, in which she's trapped all night with a stranger with high expectations, your low-pressure event is a much more appealing option.

Make sure you avoid seeding with events that are complex, far away, or longer than a few hours. People are less likely to say yes to something if the cost of commitment is high.

Once you start seeding compelling plans into a conversation, the phone number exchange and the next meeting will occur effortlessly. Especially after you complete tomorrow's missions.

DAY

MISSION 1: The Way to Digits

The sole focus of today is the second part of the phone number exchange. So read your Day 20 Briefing and learn this useful, mostly wordless, and nearly rejection-free companion piece to seeding before moving on to Mission 2.

MISSION 2: Approach, Seed, and Exchange

Approach women today using the material you've learned so far.

Seed each conversation with a plan from your calendar, as you did yesterday.

If you hit the hook point, attempt the number close you learned today before ending the conversation.

Your mission is complete after you've either received one telephone number or approached five women. Whichever happens first.

DAY 20 BRIEFING
EXCHANGING NUMBERS

There are four things every Challenger should carry in his pockets at all times:

- gum or mints to eliminate bad breath.
- a pen to write down information.
- paper—ideally business cards, even if they're someone else's.
- condoms, because if you want to stay in the game, you have to play safe.

A lot of people collect digits on their cell phones, and that's okay. There are some fun routines for cell phone number exchanges, such as inputting a humorous phrase in her phone instead of your name, so that when you call, her display reads "Hot Tamale." But good old-fashioned pen and paper has many advantages, chief among them the following technique:

Yesterday you learned how to seed a plan into a conversation. The next step is to return to the topic when you're ending the interaction.

For example, just when the conversation is at a high point and you're about to leave, throw in something like the following, almost as an afterthought: "And make sure you check out the Sushi Nazi sometime." Short pause. "Actually, you should come along with us on Thursday because then I can finish telling you about the personality types we were discussing."

Note that adding an additional incentive to go—a "because" pretext, such as closing an open loop—further lessens the possibility of flaking or rejection.

Afterward, tell her, "Here, I'll give you my information." Women may have an autopilot response when guys ask for their number, but they'll rarely, if ever, object to taking your information.

Here's what you do next: Pull your pen and a business card (or some other small piece of paper, like a receipt) out of your pocket. Tear it in half. Then write down your name and number on one half.

Afterward, hold on to the scrap of paper with your number and hand her the blank half of the card along with the pen. She'll accept them; it would be rude not to.

Four times out of five, she'll write down her name and number. The few times when she doesn't, she'll ask, "What am I supposed to do with this?" Simply show her your half of the card with your information on it, and look at her with an expression that translates as "Duh, what else are you supposed to do with it?"

Now you have your information on your paper scrap and she has her information on her half. So just exchange the scraps. Fair is fair.

Visualize this movement and practice it a few times until it's natural and smooth.

It seems simple, and it's supposed to be.

The number exchange is not a magic trick. It won't make someone who has no interest in you suddenly give you her contact information. It's a tool to help you sail smoothly through an often awkward and precarious social ritual. I've never been rejected doing this, and I've never been given fake information. The reason is not necessarily the technique itself but the timing.

The key to making this work is simply to do it after you've hit the hook point. Once you've captured her imagination with your great conversation, flair, and personality, she'll be disappointed if you leave all of a sudden without exchanging contact information. So as long as you seem sociable and trustworthy, show her that you're more interesting or attractive than her other options, and don't try to exchange numbers too early, this transaction will proceed smoothly.

If you want to be a smart-ass—and I recommend it—once she's written down her number, tell her: "Draw a picture of yourself in case I forget what you look like." You'll be able to tell a lot about her from what she draws. Plus, it's fun.

Once you have the phone number, don't leave. Keep talking to her for a couple of minutes. If you just dash off, she'll think you were only interested in her for the number and she'll get buyer's remorse. Instead, after you've exchanged numbers, share one more anecdote to make her comfortable. If you don't know what to say, tease her about the self-portrait she just drew for you. "What's that supposed to be? An arm? Yeah, I think I see the resemblance."

Finally, remember that a phone number is not an end point in the game of attraction. It's just a resting place. In some cases, you may not need to get a phone number right away, because she'll want to spend the night with you. In other cases, you may get the phone number in the first fifteen minutes but spend hours together afterward. And every now and then, you'll make a definite plan to meet later that day and not even exchange phone numbers. Though men tend to treat obtaining a phone number like it's some sort of great victory, ultimately it's just a bookmark allowing you to pick up an interaction where you left off.

DAY

MISSION 1: Meet Your Silent Wingman

Today is an easy day.

It's also an important one.

Because today you will synthesize the information you've received so far and fit it into a larger framework of attraction, seduction, and courtship.

Your Day 21 Briefing includes a list of each step of the game you've learned, from opening a conversation to obtaining a phone number. Fill in the blanks with all the material you've successfully learned and used. When you're finished, add in any material you'd like to try. Then tear it out, photocopy it, or rewrite it on a regular sheet of paper.

Consider it your cheat sheet and silent wingman.

MISSION 2: Approach Using Your Silent Wingman

Take your completed cheat sheet, fold it, and put it in your back pocket.

Your goal today is to approach a woman (or a group containing a woman) and make it all the way from the top of the sheet to the bottom.

As long as you eventually get to the number exchange, it isn't necessary to use material from every category on your cheat sheet—or even most of them. It's simply your safety net.

As you master the game, you'll find that planned or scripted material becomes necessary only as backup, in case an interaction loses momentum or isn't progressing naturally toward the next necessary stage in creating a relationship. The best way to reach mastery is to add everything you can to your repertoire— and then, once you start experiencing success regularly, to remove as much as you can without affecting your results. In other

words, practice using your cheat sheet, so that one day you'll no longer have to rely on it at all.

MISSION 3: General Courtship Strategy

What's the master plan? Perhaps it's time I let you in on it.

If you don't know where you're going, you won't know how best to get there. So turn to the second section of your Day 21 Briefing and read the article about the big picture.

DAY 21 BRIEFING
SILENT WINGMAN WORK SHEET

Attitude and Affirmations

<u>I am relaxed, confident, playful, non-needy, unflappable, positive energy. I will let go of my outcome. I am a man who women desire and want to be around. I will learn something from everyone I meet. I am testing women to see if they meet my standards. I deserve the best.</u>

_____
_____
_____

Openers

_____
_____
_____
_____

Roots

_____
_____

_____
_____

Time Constraints

_____
_____

Waypoint

<u>"How do you all know each other?"</u>_____
_____

Disqualifications

_____
_____
_____
_____

Demonstrations of Value

_____
_____
_____
_____

Cold Readings

_____
_____
_____
_____

Identity Statement

_____

Stories

_____
_____
_____
_____

Events to Seed

_____
_____
_____
_____

Number Exchange Techniques

_____
_____
_____

THE ANATOMY OF ATTRACTION

In the old days, my courtship strategy was simply to hang in there and be the last man standing. So I would make sure that either she was talking or I was talking at all times, and then hope that after enough hours and alcohol had gone by, I'd be able to make my move.

Once I worked up the courage to lunge for the kiss, though, I'd get the dreaded cheek turn. This was usually followed by a short speech explaining that she didn't want to ruin our friendship. It felt like a dagger plunging into my heart every time.

I couldn't figure out what I was doing wrong. I just thought I wasn't attractive or confident enough. And I'd repeat the same ineffectual strategy every time I had the opportunity to go out with a new woman, hoping that this one would like me.

When I discovered that attraction was a learnable skill, I quickly realized what should have been obvious to me the whole time: that every love story needs a plot. Two strangers must go through a specific sequence of events if a sexual or romantic relationship is going to build between them. And whether this sequence occurs through conscious effort or just naturally on its own, almost all relationships follow it.

I grew up thinking that one stage—building rapport—was the whole picture, which explains why I kept getting stuck in the friend zone. Friendships are built on rapport, trust, and common interests. What I didn't realize is that attraction can be built just as easily, but using different materials.

Once I understood this, everything changed. Eventually, as my interactions with women changed from friendships to romances, I was able to create a map and a clear route from the beginning of the courtship to the end. And as long as I knew where she was on that map and how to bring her to the next checkpoint, I no longer had to fear the dreaded cheek turn.

There were only five checkpoints:

1. *Open:* Every romance begins with two strangers meeting. This is how your parents met. This is how their parents met. And this is why the first nine days of the Challenge were dedicated to the minutiae of the approach, enabling you to break the ice in the most rejection-free way possible.

2. *Demonstrate value:* Once you've opened, your goal is to hit the hook point as soon as possible. Depending on the woman, her options, her self-esteem, and her interests and preferences, demonstrating value can involve as little effort as saying hello, or as much as making yourself seem like the most coveted person in the room while captivating her and her friends with powerful non-needy routines that display your worth and excellence.

3. *Create an emotional connection:* Sure, you're cool and interesting. But you could be talking to anyone in the room. Why her? It's time

to show that the two of you are bonded in some way, have things in common, click, understand each other, and were meant to meet.

4. *Structure a call to action:* Just because she likes you, that doesn't mean she's going to sleep with you. A window of possible intimacy has opened, but if you want her to jump through it, you'll have to give her an incentive to do so in the moment. Most commonly, this is done by arousing her through talk or touch. Time, comfort, trust, and laughter can also accomplish this. But sometimes she needs a stronger reason to make that physical leap. These techniques— eliciting jealousy, giving mixed messages, or even disappearing for a little while—will help her realize that if she doesn't move fast, she may lose her one opportunity to get together with you.

5. *Make a physical connection:* Once she's interested in going further, all you have to do is avoid making any mistakes that will cause her to change her mind—and walk with her across the bridge to physical intimacy in a way that doesn't make her uncomfortable, cause her to feel used, or elicit any other negative autopilot response.

Keep in mind that not every courtship starts at the beginning phases. Sometimes the interaction starts later in the process—if, for example, she's already attracted to you. In the future, you may even get to the level where you can sometimes walk up to a woman and make out with her within minutes. The better you get, the faster you'll be able to move through these stages.

A CLOSE-UP VIEW

The steps above helped guide me through nearly every approach I made. However, there are other ways to portray the same process. And different people respond better to different models.

So I sat down with the Stylelife coaches and asked them to come up with their own version for you, going into greater detail. There are six phases in their model. Here's what it looks like:

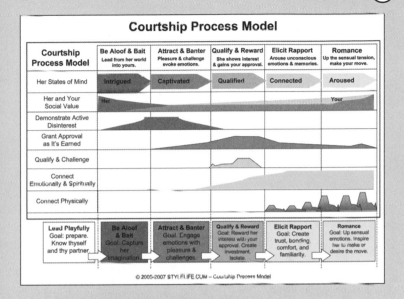

This model applies to both men meeting women and women meeting men. Each phase develops to an important milestone or turning point, allowing the relationship to advance to the next phase.

While understanding these phases in a developing relationship is helpful, knowing how to smoothly and successfully advance through them is much more useful. So I asked the team to break the phases into further detail and suggest specific actions to take and attitudes to have at each point in the process. Here's what they came up with:

Courtship Process Strategy

Courtship Phase	Goal State	Strategy: What to do When
Self-image: Lead Playfully Goal: Prepare yourself. Know yourself, your ideal partner, and outline of the plan.	Confident	Develop your assets into your identity.
		Identify your demographic of potential partners.
		Develop and know yourself and your strategy.
		Master your inner self; be a playful leader.
Phase 1: Be Aloof & Bait Goal: Capture her imagination. Get her thinking about you as an integral part of her world.	Intrigued	Appear as the object of desire, but be aloof.
		Approach nonthreateningly, time constraint.
		Ready to leave, actively disinterested, disqualify.
		Create intrigue & curiosity, inspire her to engage.
Phase 2: Attract & Banter Goal: Create pleasure & challenges to engage her emotions. Generate attraction.	Captivated	Prove your social value, create intense emotions.
		Create light confusion, challenge, tease, banter.
		Reach the hook point, win over her friends.
		Demonstrate social proof, increase social value.
		Create opportunity for quality alone time together.
Phase 3: Qualify & Reward Goal: Reward her with your approval for her interest. Create investment in you.	Qualified	See her potential, challenge her efforts.
		Qualify and challenge.
		Reward, establish commonalities, show interest.
		Cold read, control frame, reframe if needed.
Phase 4: Elicit Rapport Goal: Create trust, deep bonds, comfort, and the feeling you've known each other in the past and future. Your encounter is special and meant to be.	Connected	Entertain with stories and games.
		Change locations, create new experiences.
		Demonstrate trust, relationship telescopes time.
		Elicit core values, recall rapport memories.
		Associate with positive feelings.
		Deepen bond and connection.
		Test kinesthetically and escalate.
		Insinuate and motivate so she pursues you.
Phase 5: Romance Goal: Turn up the sensual tension and physical emotions. Inspire her to make or desire the first move.	Aroused	Create a sensual atmosphere.
		Elicit sensual values & create erotic state of mind.
		Employ erotic kinesthetic teasers and escalate.
		Observe and respond to what turns her on.
		Make the bold move, indirect sensory explosion.
		Cuddle and chill together without rushing.
		No regrets; she feels good about her decision.
		Set and manage expectations.

© 2005-2007 STYLELIFE.COM – Courtship Process Strategy

You don't need to memorize all these phases and strategies, as long as you understand their subtext—that attraction isn't random, seduction isn't something that just happens, and courtship doesn't have to involve fumbling. The fact is, whether other men are using it consciously or not, there is a formula that makes a select few of them successful with women and in life.

You now have that formula.

DAY

MISSION 1: Learn to Flip the Script

Today is frame-control day, in which you'll learn techniques to stay dominant in a conversation. These concepts will not only be of use in nearly every social situation, but they may just change the way you look at the world.

Your first task: Read all about them in your Day 22 Briefing before proceeding to the rest of today's missions.

MISSION 2: Constructive Reframing

Your first mission is to reframe negativity into positivity at least once over the course of the day.

When you hear a friend, colleague, or stranger complain or say something negative, try to reframe it into something positive. For example, if a friend says that he's incompetent at something, tell him that he just likes to do things perfectly.

If someone says, "My girlfriend is driving me crazy," respond, "Why do you think she nags? It's only because she cares. If she didn't care, she wouldn't nag."

Keep reframing until the person accepts one of your positive conclusions

If you don't hear anything negative all day, then call a friend or relative, ask what his or her biggest complaint or annoyance has been this week, and reframe that into something positive.

MISSION 3: Flirtatious Reframing

Choose from one of the following two flirtatious reframing exercises. Your mission is complete when you've performed it successfully one time. When you say these, make sure you're smiling and it's clear that you're not serious:

1. Reframe an accident into an intention: Go to a crowded place, such as a popular bar or store. When someone bumps into you or brushes against you as she walks past, jokingly say with mock indignation, "Did you just grope me? You know, I'm not that easy. I require dinner and a movie first."

2. Reframe kindness into self-interest: Go to a CD store and talk to a female employee or customer. Ask for advice on a good CD to play in the background at a dinner party—something new and cool. When she suggests a CD, teasingly accuse her of being paid to say it. "You really think I should get *that* CD? Hey, you're not getting a kickback from the record label, are you? You probably get, like, a washing machine or something for every hundred copies you sell." Then consider buying the CD. You'll find out why on Day 24.

MISSION 4: When the Going Gets Tough

If you haven't successfully exchanged phone numbers yet, study your silent wingman, put it in your back pocket, make sure your calendar is up to date, and approach four more women or groups today.

DAY 22 BRIEFING
CHANGING THE FRAME

By Thomas Scott McKenzie

An artist frames a painting. A carpenter frames a house. Project managers establish a time frame for getting work done. A criminal evades capture by framing a stranger. A film director frames a shot. Bowlers get ten frames a game.

There are dozens of different interpretations of the word *frame,* but most of them have to do with a structure or an agenda. In *Introducing NLP,* their classic book on neurolinguistic programming, authors Joseph O'Connor and John Seymour define frames as "the way we put things into different contexts to give them different meanings; what we make important at the moment."

In other words, a frame is the context through which a person, thing, or environment is perceived, and framing is a way that you can shape an interaction to achieve the result you desire. You can change your own frame, someone else's frame, or the frame in which a certain conversation or situation seems to exist.

Reframing is the process of changing the frame or providing a new view. "Reframing literally means to put a new or different frame around some image or experience," Robert Dilts writes in his book on the subject, *Sleight of Mouth.* "Psychologically, to 'reframe' something means to transform its meaning by putting it into a different framework or context than it has previously been perceived."

In fact, most kinds of flirting really amount to reframing. For example, if a woman bumps into you and you ask, "Did you just grab my ass?"—you've just reframed the situation from an accidental collision to a sexually charged situation.

Most social rules can also be thought of in terms of frames. The alpha male, for example, is the person with the dominant frame (or point of view) in a given situation. Dominance, however, should not be confused with being stubborn or a control freak. As Dilts asserts, "The person with the most flexibility will be the one who directs the interaction."

When you first meet a woman, it's important to have a strong frame, so that she feels a need to seek your approval, rather than the other way around. This is one of the reasons you're filling your Stylelife calendar with events: so that the woman can enter your world.

Even most of the things you're not supposed to do when approaching— such as acts of supplication, like buying a woman drinks so she'll talk to you— can be seen as evidence of having a weak frame or giving in to someone else's frame.

Reframing Techniques

Though there are innumerable techniques for reframing, in *Sleight of Mouth* Robert Dilts focuses on four specific ones.

CHANGING FRAME SIZE

Dilts uses the movie *Cabaret* as an example of how frame size affects our perception. One scene in the film begins with a close-up of "an angelic-looking young boy who is singing in a beautiful voice," he writes. But as the camera pulls back, viewers notice that he's dressed as a soldier. As it pulls back a little farther, viewers see his arm—and on it, an armband with a swastika.

"As the frame size gets larger and larger, we eventually see that the boy is singing at a huge Nazi rally," Dilts concludes. "The meaning and feeling conveyed by the image is completely changed by the information coming from the changes in the frame size of the image."

So during your interactions with women, imagine that you have a movie camera and can control the frame size. Let's say that you want a woman to leave the bar and go home with you, but she's worried about what her friends will think. Her frame is the equivalent of a group shot in your movie. You can zoom way out and tell her that her time on this planet is short, that adventures she'll always remember are awaiting her, and that if she constantly inhibits herself based on the opinions of others, life will pass her by. Or you can zoom into a close-up, cutting her friends out of the picture and focusing on just her wishes and desires, creating an intimate world between the two of you that she doesn't want to leave.

CONTEXT REFRAMING

Context reframing is based on the fact that the same event will have different implications depending on the circumstances or environment in which it occurs. "Rain, for example, will be perceived as an extremely positive event to a group of people who have been suffering from a severe drought, but as a negative event for a group of people who are in the midst of a flood, or who have planned an outdoor wedding," Dilts writes. "The rain itself is neither 'good' nor 'bad.' The judgment related to it has to do with the consequence it produces within a particular context."

This is useful to your inner game as well as your outer game. Let's say that you've just tried a new opener, but the woman gave you a funny look and walked away. In the context of trying to get a phone number, you would view the interaction as a failure. But if you reframe the context so your goal wasn't to obtain the digits but to determine the effectiveness of your new opener, then the interaction was a success.

CONTENT REFRAMING

Content reframing acknowledges that people see the same thing differently based on their personal attitudes, likes, dislikes, needs, and values. Dilts uses the example of an empty field of grass. A farmer sees it as an opportunity to plant crops, an architect sees it as a lot to build a Gothic home, a man flying a small plane that's running out of fuel sees the field as an emergency landing strip.

We all see things differently. Reframing based on content means looking at each individual's perspective and the intention behind his or her external behavior.

So, suppose you're back at that bar with the woman you want to take home. But her friend keeps telling her, "You guys should just stay here. Why do you need to go anywhere else? You shouldn't leave with a guy you just met."

It would be easy to simply dismiss the friend's behavior as selfish and controlling. But try to find a positive intention in her actions. Maybe she's worried about her friend's safety. Maybe she thinks you're the kind of guy who drives a van with garbage bags taped over the windows and power tools banging around in the back.

She may seem hell-bent on frustrating you, but her behavior is actually coming from a positive place. And the quicker you understand her frame, the better you can handle the objection. For example, you can deal with the situation by spending some time talking with the friend so that she trusts you more, and then giving her your phone number. This way, if she's worried about her friend or wants to find out where she is, she has the option of calling you.

REFRAMING CRITICS AND CRITICISM

The problem with critics is that they don't just point out what you're doing wrong. They often point out what they think is wrong with you.

To deal with critics, it's important to get beyond the negativity and realize that their judgments are usually made with good intentions.

This also applies to your criticisms of others. When a friend offers an idea, for example, avoid responding with something negative that could start an argument like, "That'll never work." Instead, ask a positive, constructive question that he or she won't take personally, such as "How are you going to pull that off?"

This type of reframing also works well on your fiercest critic: you. Take any excuse you may have that keeps you from achieving your goals, such as "I don't have time," and turn it into a solvable problem: "I don't use my time efficiently." Then turn that problem into a question: "How can I use my time more efficiently so that I can reach my goal?"

Reframing criticisms and limitations as "how" questions can turn a dead end into an open door.

Framing The Game

The more you learn about frames, the more flexibility, fun, and success you'll have in your social and professional life. At the very least, always keep in mind the following three things when interacting with women:

1. Always keep a strong frame. Have her meet you in your reality, rather than changing yourself to fit into hers. More than money and looks, this attitude will help you convey status.

2. Reframing is the key to both persuasion and flirtation. It gives you control of a conversation, with the ability to redirect it somewhere humorous, positive, exciting, or, at the right time, sexual. Practice it as much as you can, and not only will you become more successful with women, you'll become a more talented speaker and better-rounded thinker as well.

3. Use these techniques in moderation. Do not become obsessed with controlling the frame in every interaction all the time. Sometimes surrender can be victory.

DAY

23

MISSION 1: Self-assessment

Welcome to your final review day.

Below are a few of the skills you've learned so far. Rate yourself by circling a number from 1 to 10 in each area, with 1 being completely deficient, 5 being average, and 10 being perfect in the skill or trait listed.

Posture	1	2	3	4	5	6	7	8	9	10
Vocal Projection	1	2	3	4	5	6	7	8	9	10
Vocal Tonality	1	2	3	4	5	6	7	8	9	10
No Vocal Pausers	1	2	3	4	5	6	7	8	9	10
Grooming	1	2	3	4	5	6	7	8	9	10
Clothing Style	1	2	3	4	5	6	7	8	9	10
Inner Game	1	2	3	4	5	6	7	8	9	10
Eye Contact	1	2	3	4	5	6	7	8	9	10
Energy Level/Positivity	1	2	3	4	5	6	7	8	9	10
Approaching Strangers	1	2	3	4	5	6	7	8	9	10
Using Openers	1	2	3	4	5	6	7	8	9	10
Time Constraints	1	2	3	4	5	6	7	8	9	10
Rooting	1	2	3	4	5	6	7	8	9	10
Disqualifiers	1	2	3	4	5	6	7	8	9	10
Expressing a Unique Identity	1	2	3	4	5	6	7	8	9	10
Demonstrating Value	1	2	3	4	5	6	7	8	9	10
Non-neediness	1	2	3	4	5	6	7	8	9	10
Storytelling	1	2	3	4	5	6	7	8	9	10
Cold Reading	1	2	3	4	5	6	7	8	9	10
Spontaneous Conversation	1	2	3	4	5	6	7	8	9	10

Open Loops	1	2	3	4	5	6	7	8	9	10
Seeding	1	2	3	4	5	6	7	8	9	10
Exchanging Numbers	1	2	3	4	5	6	7	8	9	10
Frame Control/Dominance	1	2	3	4	5	6	7	8	9	10
Reframing	1	2	3	4	5	6	7	8	9	10

Select the areas in which you ranked yourself the lowest and work on those today, using the material and exercises already provided.

The final dash to get a date begins next week, so make sure you're caught up.

MISSION 2: Get a Lifeline

If you still haven't received a phone number, that's okay. One of two things is probably happening.

The first is that you've hit a sticking point. If so, it's time to get a helping hand. Go to www.stylelife.com/challenge and enter the Challenger forum. Start a thread there with the title "Sticking Point." Discuss the specific area where you're having trouble, providing as much detail as possible. Using the advice you get from coaches and fellow Challengers online, make four more approaches today.

The second possibility is that you've just been reading the book and haven't been doing the field assignments. Shame on you.

If you have already received a phone number or been on a date, don't just sit there and gloat. Go out and make four more approaches as well. Practice makes perfect.

MISSION 3: Start Persuading

Now that you know what works when meeting women, it's important to understand why these techniques work, so that you can best respond to the fluctuations, surprises, and unexpected circumstances that occur in nearly every social situation. So turn to your Day 23 Briefing, read the book report on *Influence* by Robert Cialdini, and fill in the blanks.

DAY 23 BRIEFING
THE ENGINE OF YES—A BOOK REPORT

In *Influence: The Psychology of Persuasion*, psychology professor Robert B. Cialdini examines the shortcuts that people use to make decisions, then distills the tactics of persuasion to six key psychological principles.

Cialdini's focus is on sales and advertising. However, his principles help explain not just what makes people buy a particular car or brand of soap, but also how people make decisions about each other.

Below is a brief summary of Cialdini's principles. Each has scores of applications to the process of creating attraction. For example, the principle of social proof explains why women are more attracted to men who are accompanied by other women than men who are alone. After each principle, write down at least one practical way you could employ it to improve your game.

A word of warning: These are powerful principles, and they should be used to appeal to the nobler side of people, not to their weaknesses. Steer people in the direction of their own best interests, not just yours.

Social Proof

This is the principle of majority rule: If a lot of people are doing something, others tend to believe it must be the right thing to do. As Cialdini explains, "One means we use to determine what is correct is to find out what other people think is correct."

Social proof is particularly persuasive, he notes, when the person trying to make a decision is uncertain or in an unclear situation. It's also more powerful when the individuals we're observing are people we relate to or believe are just like ourselves.

APPLICATION: _____
_____
_____

Liking

Perhaps the most obvious of them all, the principle of liking holds that we're more inclined to agree to the requests of someone we know and like.

Cialdini cites several factors that produce liking. These occur when someone has a similar fashion style, background, or interest as us; gives us compliments; is physically attractive; or has repeated contact with us, especially in situations where we have to cooperate with him or her to achieve a mutual benefit.

Cialdini adds an interesting twist to this principle: "an innocent association with either bad things or good things will influence how people feel about us." For better or worse, he continues, "If we can surround ourselves with success that we are connected with in even a superficial way . . . our public prestige will rise."

APPLICATION: _____
_____
_____
_____

Reciprocation

If people do something for us, we feel obliged to pay them back. Even "people who we might ordinarily dislike . . . can greatly increase the chance that we will do what they wish merely by providing us with a small favor prior to their requests," Cialdini writes.

An interesting corollary, he adds, is that in order to get someone to agree to a small request, a good tactic is to start by making a large request that he or she is likely to turn down.

APPLICATION: _____
_____
_____
_____

Commitment and Consistency

When people make up their mind about something, they tend not to change it—especially if they back it up with an action or a statement. Even when confronted with facts to the contrary, they often won't change their decision or belief.

"Once we have made a choice or taken a stand," Cialdini explains, "we will encounter personal and interpersonal pressures to behave consistently with that commitment."

There are many corollaries to this rule. One is that people often observe their actions in order to determine their beliefs, instead of letting their beliefs guide their actions. Another states that if you can get people to commit to the decision to buy something, but the price rises or the rules change before they have a chance to purchase it, they'll still want it. And, finally, there's the foot-in-the-door technique: To get people to commit to a large purchase, have them first make a small, inconsequential one.

APPLICATION: _____

_____

_____

_____

Authority

This principle states simply that we tend to be obedient to authority figures, even at times when their wishes make no sense or conflict with our personal beliefs.

One side effect of this, Cialdini notes, is that we're as suggestible to people who merely possess symbols of authority as we are to legitimate authorities. The symbols we often kowtow to include professional titles; uniforms or formal attire; expensive status symbols; and commanding or convincing speaking voices. We even tend to accept as an authority someone who's simply larger than us.

APPLICATION: _____

_____

_____

_____

Scarcity

According to the rule of scarcity, people perceive things that are rare, or becoming rare, as more valuable and desirable than they would if they were readily accessible. "Opportunities seem more valuable to us when their availability is limited," Cialdini notes.

One of the most important conclusions Cialdini draws from this is that "the idea of potential loss plays a large role in human decision making." Thus, when obstacles are placed in the way of something or our access to it becomes limited, our desire for it becomes greater. We then tend to assign more positive qualities to it in order to justify the desire.

"Because we know that things that are difficult to possess are typically better than those that are easy to possess," he writes, "we can often use an item's availability to help us quickly and correctly decide on its quality."

He adds that we tend to desire objects whose availability is suddenly restricted, more than items that have always been scarce.

APPLICATION: _____

_____

_____

_____

The Next Level

The most powerful motivators occur when different principles of persuasion join forces—for example, when social proof combines with scarcity. "Not only do we want the same item when it is made scarce," Cialdini writes, "we want it most when we are in competition for it."

For your final exercise, write down one example of how two different principles can be combined to create a strong motivator for attraction.

APPLICATION: _____

_____

_____

_____

DAY

24

MISSION 1: Be the Party

One of the biggest mistakes men make when trying to make plans with a woman is not having a plan in the first place. "I don't know. What do you want to do?" Just may be the worst way to ask a person out.

The next worst way is asking her, "So what are you doing on Saturday?" And then inviting yourself along.

Rather than trying to glom on to her lifestyle, a better frame to have is that perhaps she's not getting everything she wants from her life and is hoping to step into someone else's exciting world. And that world just happens to be yours.

The Stylelife Challenge is not just about women, it's about lifestyle. If you can build a positive, exciting orbit of people, places, and things around yourself, one that other people respect and want to be a part of, you will meet and attract women automatically.

So to close out the Stylelife Challenge, you are going to plan a dinner party for Day 30. Your task is to read today's briefing and find out just how to pull this off before moving on to Mission 2.

MISSION 2: Seed Your Stylelife Party

Your mission today is to seed your dinner party.

Approach women and groups using the material you've learned. But instead of seeding an event in your calendar, seed your dinner party. You may want to discuss the theme or occasion for the party, and mention any friends who share something in common with her. But don't invite her.

Only when the conversation is ending, and it's time to exchange numbers, will you invite her to the party.

One way to do this is to say, "You know what? You should come to the dinner party. I think you'll really enjoy some of the people there. And, besides, we need a wild card."

If she asks what a wild card is, either tease her by saying "someone unpredictable" or compliment her by saying "someone new and interesting." What you choose to say here depends entirely on her self-esteem.

Unless she's really excited about going, don't give her the details of the party on the spot. That can come across as too eager. Wait to talk on the phone first. This way she'll have to work a little harder for it, and demonstrate that she's trustworthy and will mix well with your friends.

Your mission is complete after you've either collected the phone number of one potential party guest or made five approaches. Whichever happens first.

Tomorrow you will be using that number.

DAY 24 BRIEFING
YOUR STYLELIFE DINNER PARTY

Do you know what's great about having a party?

It's an excuse to get the phone number of nearly anyone you meet, as well as an excuse to call anyone you haven't talked to in a long time. No number will ever go stale as long as you have the occasional dinner party.

For the purposes of the Challenge, the definition of a party is simply six or more people gathering in any public or private location for the purposes of a fun, recreational, bonding experience.

Intent

Having a dinner party allows you to get together with a woman on your turf, where she has to compete for your attention. It also makes for an easy, low-commitment date. There are plenty of people around to keep the conversation going and build the anticipation you both will have for private time together later.

Furthermore, having a regular party will add to your circle of friends and potential girlfriends; build your social skills; strengthen your leadership qualities; and help you develop the kind of lifestyle others want to be a part of. Some of the most desired women in the world don't just date actors, musicians, directors, billionaires, and athletes, they also date club owners and promoters. This is because everyone wants to be accepted by the in-crowd. So do them all a favor by creating an in-crowd and accepting them.

Promotion

You don't need to create invitations for your dinner party. And, whatever you do, don't make flyers for your party. This is a small, exclusive event with a hand-picked guest list, and flyers imply mass, indiscriminate invitations.

You do, however, need a reason for having the party. It doesn't need to be anything complicated. Consider presenting your party to women as a weekly ritual where you gather some of the most interesting people you've met for good food and conversation. Or, better still, actually make it a weekly or monthly ritual. You could call it Monday martini night or the Tuesday charades challenge or the Wednesday international cook-off. If you want to get really pretentious, you could even call it a salon.

Another option is to create an occasion for the dinner. If a friend of yours has done anything of note—released an independent CD, published an article, started a website, had a birthday, adopted a puppy, bought a new shirt—throw a party to honor him or her. Then play the new CD, read an excerpt of the article, or proudly display the new shirt at the party.

Another pretext is to make it a holiday. Every single day on the calendar commemorates something—national sibling day, barbershop quartet day, the birth of Gary Coleman—so throw a party to celebrate.

Location

Your party can take place at any of a number of locations.

The best venue is your house or apartment, or the house or apartment of a friend. There are only a few necessary preparations you need to make: cleaning the space, providing something to eat, selecting appropriate music, and—assuming you and your guests are of legal age—having enough alcohol to last throughout the party.

If cooking isn't your forte, a dinner party can be an excuse for you to learn. If one of the women you've met enjoys cooking, convince her to help out. Since your guests know you're throwing the party to teach yourself to cook, they won't even mind when the turkey catches fire. As long as there's alcohol to drink.

If you don't have the time or incentive to cook, just order out food, remove it from the to-go containers, leave it warming in the oven until the guests arrive, then serve it in regular dishes. If no one asks, you don't need to tell them it's from the Greek restaurant down the street.

If the gathering is fewer than ten people, provide an enclosed sitting space to facilitate conversation. Buy cheap folding chairs if you have to. If you're less experienced in hosting, start or end the night with a group event, such as a favorite weekly television show or an interactive game like charades. Never underestimate the appeal of anything that was fun at age seven.

The second-best venue is a lounge or restaurant that has tables or couches large enough for your entire group. Make a reservation in advance and confirm it on the day of the party. It's perfectly fine for everyone to split the bill. Though in reality it's no different from a regular dinner out, your intent to celebrate as a group is enough to justify calling it a party.

Other locations include a park or beach for an evening picnic or barbecue; a bar or club; even a bowling alley, hotel room, or amusement park. Your only limits are your imagination and the law.

Casting

You're not going to throw some kind of blow-out keg party, unless you really want to. Most likely, it'll be a small dinner party for a select group—and that's how you're going to explain it to the woman you're talking to. The more select and exclusive your party appears to be, the better it will turn out and the quicker word will get around town.

For example, rather than saying you're inviting people, tell her that you're "casting" the dinner party—picking and choosing just the right combination of interesting personalities, interests, and occupations—and she might make a good addition to the cast. After all, every party needs a wild card.

Though calling her a wild card can be a fun tease, you actually will want one at your party. So make sure you invite someone whose conversation or behavior is slightly eccentric and outgoing (but not unpleasant or extreme). It takes the pressure off you as a host, because the guests will have someone else to talk about and entertain them.

You'll also want to invite at least one male friend who's a good conversationalist, at least one female friend or couple, and the women you've met (or will meet) during the Challenge. It is crucial to make sure there's more than one woman present at your party, so that the girl you're interested in doesn't feel uncomfortable or outnumbered.

If more than one woman you met during the Challenge shows up, don't worry if they compare notes on how they met you. Just keep your frame strong: You're a social person who enjoys going out and meeting new people, discussing whatever's on your mind with them, and bringing them together to network. If you live in this reality, they'll usually end up competing for you.

If she wants to bring a friend, don't panic. Let her. If you charm her friend, you're likely to charm her as well. Even if it's a male friend, that's okay. After all, you've invited other women, and those women can even help keep him occupied. Though you don't want to encourage her to bring friends, if she does, it will only widen your social circle and make the next party that much better.

If you're having the dinner party at a home, the energy can sometimes dip after the meal. One way to prevent this from happening is to invite a second shift of four to eight people for cocktails afterward. The new faces, enthusiasm, and energy will give the party the spark it needs to make it lively and memorable. (Be careful about the timing: most guests arrive roughly a half hour after the time you tell them the party starts.)

For each person you invite, make sure that you have an interesting way to introduce him or her—consider using the same kind of identity statement you made for yourself. The better you make your friends look, the better you look.

Connecting

There are several things you can do before, during, and after the party to deepen your connection with the woman you're interested in.

If the party is at your home, have her stay and help you clean up. If the party is elsewhere, think of somewhere to go afterward.

Sometimes it can be fun to get her involved in helping out with the party, rather than just relying on your work and hospitality. To do this, give her tasks or assignments, such as bringing or cooking food.

One friend of mine makes sangria with his dates. The work is light, it involves alcohol, and it's perfect for two people. To do this, get a bottle of Spanish wine, two limes, two lemons, two oranges, a mango, and a half cup of sugar. Pour the wine in a pitcher, let it breathe for ten minutes, then add the sugar. Squeeze the juice of a lime, lemon, and orange into the wine. Have her slice up the rest of the fruit into wedges and add it to the drink. Refrigerate it for an hour if possible, toss in a tray's worth of ice cubes, and pour it for your guests. (This recipe serves five people, so double it if you have ten guests.)

Other activities to do together range from shopping for ingredients (the grocery store can be a fun first date) to attempting to roll your own sushi, which can get messy—and that's a good thing.

Be careful not to dote on her too much or bend over backward to keep her entertained. And don't get jealous if another guy at the party starts talking to your date. As the host, you're the man of the moment; no one is a threat to you. If you have a trusted friend, let him know your identity statement, so he can share his admiration of you with your date.

The goal of the dinner party is to have a good time, build an exciting lifestyle, and bring together people who will find one another interesting. If you can accomplish this, the attraction will take care of itself.

DAY

25

MISSION 1: Phone Rules

The step after exchanging numbers—calling—is a source of anxiety for some men. However, the rule of phone engagement is simple: Don't do anything wrong. She's only just met you, and one warning signal is the only excuse she needs to decide never to see you again.

You don't want that to happen. So your task is to read the Day 25 Briefing on phone game.

MISSION 2: Plan Your Party

If you haven't settled on a location for your dinner party on Day 30, do so.

Write down your ideal guest list of six to ten people below. Include any women you've exchanged numbers with. Write each person's name in the column on the left and his or her identity in the column on the right. Your description of each person should be terse and compelling, so that when you scan this list, the party looks like a special event.

Name	Identity
1.	
2.	
3.	
4.	
5.	
6.	
7.	
8.	

MISSION 3: Harvest Your Seeds

Phone all the women whose numbers you've collected in the last few weeks. Practice the telephone techniques you learned in your briefing.

Invite each woman to the event or party you've planned for Day 30. Make sure you give her a specific location and time to arrive. Emphasize that it's going to be a small, handpicked group, so she knows her invitation is a privilege and her presence is crucial to the mix.

Compared to asking complete strangers for movie recommendations on the phone, this should be a piece of cake.

If you haven't yet received a phone number, make five more approaches today, with the goal of party recruitment in mind. Make sure you study your cheat sheet first.

If you've already been on a date, don't forget to add your name to the winner's circle on the Stylelife forum and share the story with your fellow Challengers.

DAY 25 BRIEFING
PHONE GAME

You know, I used to wait two days to call anybody, but now it's like everyone in town waits two days. So I think three days is kind of money. What do you think?
—FROM THE FILM *SWINGERS*

So you've had a successful approach and exchanged numbers with a woman you really like, but now what? What if she's forgotten you? What if you're too nervous on the phone and blow it? What if she's busy on the day you want to see her? What if she's in the middle of something more important when she answers? What if a guy picks up the phone? What if she's given you a wrong number? What if California falls into the ocean?

Don't worry about it.

If you relax, the first phone call can be a very simple process.

How Long to Wait

How long are you supposed to wait between getting the number and making the call?

Some say phone the next day; others say wait three days.

They're all wrong. There is no fixed amount of time that needs to pass.

Rather, here's how long you can wait: as long as you possibly can.

In other words, if you meet a woman and make an amazing connection, and she begs you to call her, you can wait as long as a week. She's not going to forget you.

However, if you meet a woman, talk for a few minutes, exchange numbers, and afterward see her talking to different guys all night, you're going to have to call her the next day. This is because, if you didn't make that deep a connection or impression, within forty-eight hours she's likely to have forgotten all about you.

When it comes to call times, the general rule is: Don't lose the momentum. Call her while the interaction is still fresh in her head, but not so soon and so often that she thinks you're a stalker.

To Block or Not to Block?

Many so-called experts advise blocking your phone number when calling a woman. They also suggest that you not leave a message if she doesn't pick up.

The idea, they explain, is that if you keep calling, eventually she'll answer—and once you've trapped her, you can convince her to see you.

I don't use or recommend this crowbar method, unless you're a telemarketer.

The fact is: If she's not calling you back or taking your calls, the problem is not your phone game; it's your approach game, because you didn't convey the qualities necessary for her to want to see you again. In fact, whenever something goes wrong at one stage in the interaction, it generally means you made a mistake in the previous stage.

So never block your calls and always leave a message. Why? Because it shows confidence. If you displayed an attractive personality, demonstrated your value, and conveyed trust when you first met her, she's going to be excited when you call.

Your goal should be to leave every interaction with the woman worrying, "What if he doesn't call?"

If you've seeded your event properly, when you do phone, she'll know just what you're calling about and she'll be comfortable taking the call.

What to Say

Here's a general structure to follow on the first phone call:

1. Try to avoid introducing yourself by name. Instead, begin the conversation with a callback to your previous conversation. If you used the Village People opener to meet her, when she picks up, say slowly and confidently, "So I found out: There's no fireman in the Village People." She'll know who it is. If you teased her by calling her a brat, when she picks up, just say, "Hey, brat." This way, instead of reminding her that you're a stranger (especially if she happens to have forgotten your name), you bring her back to the good time she originally had talking with you.

2. To avoid an awkward pause, after she greets you, launch into a quick story from your life. Select an appropriate narrative you created on storytelling day, or add a new one to your repertoire. Begin by saying something like "The most amazing thing happened to me today . . ." Just make sure your story is short, and that the point of it isn't to build yourself up but to make her smile, laugh, and feel comfortable.

3. Speak in a deep, calm, comfortable voice tinged with fun and positive energy. It's good to be upbeat, but don't talk too fast or be too hyper. Smile on the phone, and she'll hear it.

4. After telling your short story, give her a chance to speak. Most of the time she'll tell you about her day or ask a question. If she doesn't, just move on.

5. Make plans for later in the week. Some experts suggest saying what days you're busy first to demonstrate, among other things, that you have a full life and are squeezing her into it. Incorporating the push-pull you learned on disqualification day, you might say something like "I'm busy Friday and Saturday, but I'm having a small dinner party on Sunday. I'm casting a group of really interesting people, and you should come. We need a troublemaker."

6. If you're inviting her to an event other than your party, don't frame the interaction as a date. Invite her to "hang out," "tag along," or "join" you and your friends.

7. If she says she can make it, great. If she's busy, let her know about one of the other events on your calendar. And only one. Unless she gushes with enthusiasm to go, tell her that she'd probably enjoy it and if a space frees up, you'll call her and let her know.

8. Whether or not she's available, don't suddenly say good-bye and hang up after inviting her out. Just as you did after exchanging phone numbers, continue the conversation for another minute or two. Add a little playful banter or share a quick, related story.

9. End on a high note. Be the person who says good-bye first. You're busy. You've got things to do.

Though this script is simple and has been used effectively by thousands of men, it's not the only way to handle the first phone call. As you become more comfortable with the process, you may want to distinguish yourself from other men by calling first just to talk briefly and then making plans on the second call.

If you prefer to text, try to avoid it for your first interaction. On the other hand, if you fall into the trap of phone tag before having your first conversation, texting can save the day.

If She's Too Busy Again . . .

If she's vague about committing to plans or turns down multiple invitations, it's time to examine your game. At some point in the initial interaction, you probably made a mistake. Perhaps you conveyed lower social value, came across as desperate, or exchanged phone numbers too early. Maybe your sense of style (or lack thereof) didn't fit her dating criteria. Figure out what your shortcoming was and work to improve it. In a few rare cases, if you're doing everything right but she's still flaky, she may have a boyfriend or be getting over one.

In general, never accept the words "too busy" as a regular excuse. If Angelina Jolie called and invited you to a dinner she's having at her mansion with Bono, Jay-Z, Bill Clinton, and George Lucas, would you be able to make it?

Of course you would. You'd break whatever plans you had, blow off work, and probably walk there on your hands if you had to.

Your goal in every interaction is to be so interesting and such a rare find that she's never too busy for you. After all, if you met the perfect 10, wouldn't you manage to find time for her?

So be the perfect 10.

DAY

MISSION 1: Clear Your Mind

This may be the most challenging day so far, but it will also provide the greatest benefit to your intuitive understanding of the game.

Your first task: Forget everything you've learned so far.

MISSION 2: Approach Unarmed

Approach three women or groups today—using no material.

Do not start the conversation by asking for an opinion. Do not use scripted disqualifiers. Do not discuss rings and Greek gods. Do not tear business cards in half.

Improvise something—perhaps about someone around you or an item she's wearing or whatever's on your mind at the time—to start the conversation. Don't be afraid of small talk; asking generic questions about work, movies, and travel; or even buying her a drink if you're in a bar or a café. Break all the rules.

Stay in the conversation until she excuses herself, or it's clear that she wants you to leave. It may get awkward, but hang in there.

If possible, time the interaction. Your goal is to stay in the conversation for at least ten minutes without using material.

If all goes well, feel free to invite her to your dinner party or one of your calendar events.

MISSION 3: Live the Difference

Reflect on your approaches today.

Did you notice any differences between using material and freestyling? Any differences between how you interacted before the Stylelife Challenge versus now? If so, write them in the space below.

_____

_____

_____

_____

_____

MISSION 4: Fill-ins

Your final task today is to read the following advice on filling in the gaps:

There's a sticking point that some Challengers hit around this point. They approach a group, open, demonstrate value, cold read—they do it all. Yet inside they feel tense and awkward, because they have no idea what to do *between* all these techniques. What do they say? How do they transition from piece to piece? How do they get to a point where they can exchange phone numbers?

These are, of course, irrational fears—after all, they've managed to have interesting conversations with people before. Overcoming material dependency, and realizing that you have plenty of things to say to fill in the gaps is one of the goals of today's field assignment.

It can be easy to forget that it's your personality, more than the material, that will make her want to see you again. Routines are great because they show you to be more interesting than most guys. They also serve as springboards to get you to the next stage in an interaction. But your entire conversation doesn't need to be one big performance. You don't want the woman to think of you as a monkey in a little hat, turning the crank on a music box for her entertainment.

So stay up-to-date on entertainment, culture, current events, and happenings around town; cultivate the ability to pay attention to the details of what other people do, say, and wear; master the art of social intelligence; get comfortable in your own skin; and, if you're still having a problem filling in the gaps, take improv comedy courses to learn spontaneity.

If the game is self-improvement, then we're all in it for life. So learn to play it right.

DAY

MISSION 1: Learn to Connect

Imagine if you met a woman whose favorite musician and film were exactly the same as yours; who shared your strongest beliefs and opinions; and who turned out to have grown up just a block away from you, even though you'd never met. Wouldn't you feel like you'd met someone incredible?

This is the power of rapport. And it's something you want to create with every woman you're interested in. So turn to your Day 27 Briefing and read about it before moving on to the rest of today's missions.

MISSION 2: Date Your Calendar

Print or copy a fresh Stylelife calendar page.

Fill in events—as well as selling points and reasons to go—every day until the end of the Challenge. Make sure you include your party. Then familiarize yourself with the activities, the dates you listed them on, and the reasons for going.

MISSION 3: Rapport Workout

Choose two of the three rapport exercises below to perform. It's okay to try them with a coworker, cashier, casual acquaintance, or even in an online chat, but you'll get more out of the exercises if you do them with a new person or group you've approached. If the interaction goes well, make sure you invite the woman you're interested in to your dinner party or one of your calendar events.

Pay close attention to the other person's reactions as you increase and decrease your level of rapport.

MAKING AND BREAKING RAPPORT

During the following exercise, observe the other person's reaction as you instantly create rapport—and then quickly break it.

Have a conversation like the following:

YOU: Where are you from?
HER: [*Whatever city*].
YOU: Oh my God, no way! I grew up there too. What school did you go to?
HER: [*Whatever school*].
YOU: Get out of here. I went there too.
HER: Really?
YOU: No. I've never actually been there. [*Then, in a dry monotone*] Are you upset?

RAPPORT TEST

In the following exercise, break rapport and then see if the person you're talking to will strive to re-create it.

YOU: Out of curiosity, what's the last CD you bought or song you downloaded?
HER: [*Some song by some artist*].
YOU: Really? I'm surprised. I'm not the biggest fan of their music.

If she backpedals and says she doesn't really like the artist either, this means she's seeking rapport with you. If she tells you why she likes the music or disagrees with you, then either she isn't seeking rapport or she's simply confident in her taste and opinions.

PHYSICAL RAPPORT

This exercise illustrates the power of body language to affect someone else's state.

During a conversation with someone you're comfortable with, cross your arms and turn away from them while they're talking. If seated, cross your legs away from them as well. Remain in that position for a minute or two.

See if the person starts to get rattled or uncomfortable—or even comments on it. Then uncross your arms, open up your body language, and turn toward him or her again. If the person is a good friend, ask if he or she noticed or felt a difference when you broke physical rapport.

Repeat this exercise one more time today with a different person.

DAY 27 BRIEFING
THE PATH TO RAPPORT

Creating rapport is the process of developing a connection with someone based on trust, comfort, commonalities, and affinity. For many men, it's the easiest and most natural part of the courtship process.

Rapport is the point in the interaction when she sees those little parts of you that you try to hide sometimes—your inner nerd, your goofy side, your enthusiasm for superhero comics, or musical theater, or monster truck rallies—and finds them endearing. It's the moment when she shares her innermost thoughts, experiences, and feelings—and you understand them, perhaps better than anyone else she's ever met. It's when you find yourselves laughing in unison or starting to say the same thing at the same time.

In short, rapport is when two people really get to know each other and find out that, yes, they were supposed to meet. How lucky they must be.

At the same time, rapport is a castle built of Lego. It can be dismantled in an instant and put back together a few seconds later. Knowing when and how to build and break rapport will help propel an interaction through the stages necessary to create a romantic or sexual relationship.

Watch any love story. Before two lovers fully unite, they first lose rapport—maybe through a misunderstanding or a disapproving parent or a spurned rival or punishment for a mistake. They experience anguish, and then, in their sorrow, realize just how strongly they feel about the other person. Only when rapport has been regained and mutual feelings confessed do they feel complete again.

So-called nice guys make the mistake of trying only for rapport with a woman, to the exclusion of everything else that builds attraction. There's a fine line between naturally having rapport and being seen as trying too hard to get rapport.

In addition, timing is key. If you strive for rapport too early, the relationship may fall into the friend zone. If you strive for rapport too late, she may think you're a player who doesn't see her as the dynamic individual she is. The best time to build rapport when meeting a woman is after hitting the hook point but before getting too physical. Now that she's interested in you and invested in the interaction, you can even ask all the questions you were advised not to when first meeting her.

To help you create the kind of rapport that magically just happens, I've asked Stylelife senior coach Don Diego Garcia to break it down.

And he did, into two neat categories: lead and sync.

Lead

For decades, parents trusted their children to be entertained by Fred Rogers through the TV program *Mister Rogers' Neighborhood*. He started each show with a mild manner and a friendly "Hi, neighbor!"

Notice that he didn't say, "Hi, stranger!" He *assumed* you were his neighbor. Although you probably never lived anywhere near Fred, he made you feel as though you did. Mr. Rogers assumed a neighborly affinity and went about his show as though you were an old friend in his living room. It was a hit.

Though you don't want to be as exaggeratedly friendly as Mr. Rogers, you do want to assume rapport with women in a similar way. To do so, simply ask yourself this question: "How would I act if this person were a lifelong friend?" Now pass that answer through a filter of social propriety, and you'll know how to approach.

You should assume rapport from the moment she first sees or hears you. Suppose there's someone you want to meet in the dairy section of the local supermarket. An approach that assumes formality begins with you holding out your hand and introducing yourself by name.

An approach that assumes rapport, however, begins differently: "I could understand 2 percent for people who can't decide between whole and nonfat milk, but 1 percent? Is there really that big a difference between 2 percent and 1 percent?"

People also bond naturally with credible leaders who possess such qualities as confidence, authority, authenticity, security, self-assuredness, courtesy, and honesty. Staying grounded in these qualities will prevent you from succumbing to the risks of seeking rapport—such as supplication, losing your frame, falling into the friend zone, or becoming her therapist instead of her lover.

Sync

Carl Jung liked to talk about synchronicity as attaching meaning to events that are coincidental. I call the process of actively producing this state syncing.

Syncing is not copying or imitating everything your partner does. Syncing is a more subtle form of falling into pace with them and cultivating empathy. People in groups do it unconsciously all the time. When you sync correctly, your partner will bond with you more on an emotional, spiritual, and energetic level than on an intellectual level.

Let's examine the ways you can get in sync with the woman you're interested in.

VISUALLY

To sync visually with a woman, watch her posture, facial expression, breathing pace, gestures, or even blinking rate, and match them. Remain relaxed and calm as you do this. If you match her just right, she'll start subconsciously mirroring your body language as well.

AUDITORALLY

If you notice that she uses a few specific words frequently or that certain words seem to have a special meaning to her, consider them hot-button words and mentally store them for future use. You can also match your language to her work jargon, regional expressions, and any words that define her as a member of a particular subculture.

Auditory syncing can also involve paying attention to words that suggest that the speaker has a special affinity for certain senses. For example, visual people tend to use words like *focus, bright, see,* and *show* when discussing their thoughts and desires. People who live in their feelings use words like *touch, feel, aware,* and *sense.* Audiophiles prefer descriptors like *ring, sounds,* and *click.* Listen closely to her speech patterns, pick up on which sense words she uses, and then sprinkle them into your own conversation.

You can also match other things about her way of speaking—her pitch, volume, tempo, timbre, or tonality—or even her nonverbal utterances, from groans to laughter to pauses. This may sound extreme, but it's practically common sense that a slow talker and a fast talker, for example, will have a hard time communicating. The slow talker will have trouble following the fast talker, and the fast talker will be impatient with the slow talker. The more similarly you communicate, the more likely you'll get along.

LOGICALLY

Sync logically by discovering particular interests, aesthetics, morals, sensibilities, or background details you have in common. This common form of building rapport involves playing the "me too" game. Me-too topics can include family experiences, travel stories, career goals, entertainment preferences, personal idiosyncrasies, and relationship criteria.

You can sync logically with light rapport topics: where she's from, why she's out, what her interests are. Later in the interaction, move into deep rapport, using morality conundrums, personality tests, imagination exercises, confessions of vulnerability, intimate stories, and discussions of goals and dreams.

In a nutshell, similarity leads to affinity. Affinity leads to rapport.

EMOTIONALLY

As you're talking to the woman you're interested in, wholeheartedly invest yourself in understanding how she thinks and feels. Master the skill of empathy to put yourself in her place. See things from her point of view. We all want to find someone in this big, alienating, often uncaring world who understands us.

US VERSUS THEM

One of the most powerful ways to build rapport is to create a conspiracy in which only you two have something in common, and no one else gets it. This can range from bonding over a peculiar idea that few others believe to role playing and telling others that you're childhood friends or even engaged. These latter gambits are particularly powerful because the roles themselves are ones of increased rapport.

Troubleshooting

Though some of these subtle strategies may take a conscious effort at first, eventually they'll become more automatic. The best way to master them is to practice one at a time until you understand how each works. You'll notice, for example, that mirroring her breathing will subtly change the energy around the two of you and draw you closer together to the exclusion of everyone else in the room.

Often, the biggest barrier to creating wide and deep rapport is not the other person but you. If you're too scared to reveal yourself or show any vulnerability, then she typically won't feel comfortable letting down her guard with you. Rapport is a two-way street. And it doesn't exist without trust and openness.

So if you ever find it difficult to achieve rapport, whether it's because of your masks and walls or hers, consider letting your guard down, forgetting about all these techniques, and just relating to her with an open heart. You may be surprised.

DAY

28

MISSION 1: Your Internal Compass

There is one key piece of the game that most people never mention, teach, or realize exists. Even if you stop using routines and abandon the structure you've been taught, you will still be relying on this.

Beyond its uses in attraction, this is a skill that affects all areas of your life, whether you're interviewing for a job or getting held up at gunpoint.

Read about it in your Day 28 Briefing before proceeding with the rest of today's assignments.

MISSION 2: Are You a Psychic or a Psycho?

The following exercise works best with a seated group of two or more people who look easygoing.

Your assignment is to guess how they know one another. Are they related? Roommates? Friends from work or school? In a relationship? On a date? Taking a class together?

Make an educated guess. Then walk up, ask, and find out if you're correct.

Your calibration skills will not only help you guess correctly, they'll also help you pose the question in a way that doesn't make the group feel like it's part of a laboratory experiment.

For example, you can say: "You have to help me quickly settle a debate I was just having with my friend. We noticed you all talking, and he said you guys probably all work together. I guessed you were friends from college."

If they give you a funny look—which will happen occasionally—acknowledge the oddness of the situation by saying something like, "I know, strange question, but he's into psychology. He does this stuff all the time. Then I have to do the dirty work."

Make sure that you're smiling, your approach comes from a place of healthy curiosity, they know you're not asking in a judgmental way, and you use a time constraint.

Your mission is complete once you've approached three groups or made one correct guess, whichever comes first.

If the conversation goes so well that you end up joining the group for a while, take the opportunity to stock your dinner party with some new faces.

MISSION 3: Get Proof of Interest (Optional)

If Mission 2 seems too easy, or if you want to do more calibration training today, then here's an additional goal to add to your approaches above.

Your secondary mission is to receive at least one indicator of interest from a woman in one of the groups you approach. Study the list of attraction signals in today's briefing to familiarize yourself with these indicators.

If you don't receive an indicator of interest in one of the three groups you approach today, then make two more approaches using your standard opener.

Your mission is complete once you've received one indicator of interest, or you've approached five women or groups altogether today.

If you do receive any indicators of interest from a woman you've approached, then it's your duty to exchange numbers and invite her to your party.

DAY 28 BRIEFING
CALIBRATION

There are only three things you need to perfect in order to master the art of attracting women:

- Who you are
- What you do
- When and how you do it

When it comes to who you are, during the first few days of the Challenge you worked on your goals, mission statement, and identity. Tomorrow you'll drill down and refine the individual characteristics of your personality.

As for what you do, you've spent nearly every day developing that element of your game, from openers to demonstrations of value.

And, for when and how you do it, you've learned the order and sequence of each attraction event and studied the big picture. But there is one more piece to this puzzle: calibration. And it makes all the difference.

Technically speaking, calibration is the act of adjusting or correcting the accuracy of a measuring instrument, usually through determining its deviation from a standard. In terms of attraction, the definition remains the same—but the measuring instrument is you and the standard is her.

Identifying the Instrument

When approaching, calibration is the skill that allows you to read the dynamics of the group or the woman you're interested in and know what to do next.

If, for example, a woman saunters up to you in a bar, rubs your chest, and says you're cute, what do you do?

If you try an opinion opener, you'll bore her—and a demonstration of value will seem like you're trying too hard. Through calibration, you'll know to skip most of the stages you've learned and start thinking about how to give her the physical experience she's looking for. Further calibration will help you determine if she wants to make out with you right there, if she wants to be taken home, or if she's just trying to make someone else in the room jealous. All these evaluations—made in a fraction of a second—will determine your next course of action.

Calibration continues to be necessary throughout an interaction. Making slight adjustments in your body language, eye contact, and tonality can affect the behavior, responses, and interest level of the woman you're talking to. Try standing too close to her and noticing how she reacts; then stand too far away. Try leaning in, then leaning back. Explore making direct eye contact, looking at her mouth, or looking over her shoulder when talking.

Learning to read her responses, and then adjusting your actions to elicit the feelings you want her to have, is the core of the game.

Setting the Instrument

Though calibration is one of the most critical pieces of the game, it can also be a trap. If you overcalibrate and worry too much about every small sign a woman gives you, you'll probably become anxious and insecure, and sabotage the interaction.

When meeting a new person, all kinds of thoughts and snap judgments, both positive and negative, may swim through your mind in a matter of moments. So to avoid erring on the side of insecurity, when you're trying to assess how she feels about you, set your calibrator not to 0 (neutral interest) but to +2 (slightly interested). Go into every interaction with the attitude that the woman you're interested in is into you—and if you find yourself wondering how to interpret something she does, assume the best. This will motivate you to press forward with confidence.

Labeling the Instrument

After setting your instrument this way, you should then try to determine how she currently feels about you and what she needs to progress to the next stage in your attraction sequence.

At all times, you're looking for one of three responses from her:

- Green Light—A positive response, which means go forward
- Yellow Light—A neutral response, which means proceed with caution
- Red Light—A negative response, which means stop what you're doing

Red lights are the realm of damage control, when you've miscalibrated and crossed a line or made an error. If that occurs, back up to the last yellow light.

The yellow light is what you'll encounter most often. It's a point when anything can happen. And the outcome depends on your ability to assess where she is in the courtship process, where she needs to be taken next, and what she needs to get there. Among the things she may need from you are more value, more attraction, more comfort, more trust, or just more time.

Make these calculations in your mind as imperceptibly as possible. One bad habit people sometimes develop while learning the game is that they become reaction seeking. Remember, as soon as it becomes clear that you've done or said anything solely to get a particular response from her, it not only loses its impact, it also appears needy.

The game hinges on subtleties and details like these, in part because, whether she knows it or not, she's also calibrating you. And most women have far more finely tuned instruments and intuition than we do.

Reading the Instrument

Some people's calibration is a little off. They can't seem to tell when they're making people uncomfortable—or, conversely, when a woman is actually attracted to them.

No matter where you currently stand, if you pay attention and learn from the feedback a woman gives you, you'll accumulate enough experience and success that your calibration will correct itself. Eventually your intuition will become so strong that you won't need to apply any rules to calibrate. You'll just know.

In the meantime, here are a few clear signs that can help you tell whether a woman is attracted to you. These signals are subtle, so don't rely on just one to give you the green light to proceed. Make sure you have three to four clear, positive indications before assuming she's interested in getting a little more intimate. These indicators of interest include:

- She asks you, without prompting, what your name is, what you do for work, where you're from, or how old you are.
- You lean back, and she leans toward you.
- Her legs are uncrossed (or crossed toward you), her body is angled toward you, and her arms are uncrossed.
- She changes her opinion of a song, movie, or current event based on your opinion.
- You make a joke, and no one in the group laughs but her.
- You take her hand to lead her somewhere, and she squeezes it—especially if you let go and she holds on.

- She says, "I'm not going to sleep with you" or "I'm not going home with you," before you've asked her to or conveyed any intent to do so.
- She playfully punches or slaps your hand or arm.
- She ignores her friends when they try to contribute or want to leave.
- You stop talking and make eye contact, and she holds it for longer than a second.
- You turn to speak to someone else, and she waits for you to turn back to her.
- She displays a combination of subconscious attraction gestures: lip licking, hair twirling, pupil dilating, even nostril flaring.
- She grooms herself or adjusts her clothes to expose more skin while talking to you.
- She absentmindedly fondles something like a straw, cell phone, or piece of jewelry. (If she's clutching it tightly or fidgeting with it, that's not a good sign.)
- You stop talking, and she tries to continue the conversation, usually with the word "So . . ."
- She mirrors your movements—stroking her hair after you stroke yours, sipping her drink after you sip yours, even making a face after you make one at her.

Like sending out a sonar signal and waiting for it to return to determine a distance, you can send out signals to test her interest. To do this, make a small action and notice how she responds. For example, playfully (and lightly) punch her in the shoulder. If she punches or hits you back, these are good signs; if she stiffens or recoils slightly, these are not so good.

Be forewarned that some women will be very touchy-feely as soon as they meet you because they seek the validation of guys chasing them, enjoy the power it gives them over men, or are showing off for someone else in the room. With these women, don't consider anything a genuine display of interest unless you know you've earned or deserved it. Until then, tell them with a smile that you charge twenty dollars a touch, and they're racking up quite a bill.

Upgrading the Instrument

We've discussed calibrating to determine your course of action. But there's another type of calibration that's more fun and powerful. It includes elements of cold reading, determines which disqualifiers are appropriate if any, and helps build rapport.

Like using X-ray glasses, this advanced form of calibration allows you to explore her innermost thoughts, needs, and desires. To train yourself to do this, as you're talking to her, ask yourself:

- What type of personality does she have?
- Does she have high or low self-esteem?
- Is she sexually open or reserved?
- What does she do for work?
- Is she currently in a relationship?
- Is she an oldest, youngest, middle, or only child?
- Is she closer to her mother or her father?
- Is she primarily athletic, emotional, or intellectual?
- What qualities is she attracted to in men?
- What are her needs?
- Where is she in life and what is she looking for?

Just like with cold reading, there are many clues that will give you this information. They include her clothing, makeup, posture, gestures, eye movements, the way she speaks, and the people she's with.

Mastering the Instrument

There's only one way to master calibration: Get feedback.

The simplest way to practice is to turn on a soap opera and watch it with the sound off. Try to guess as much as you can about the relationship between the characters on-screen. Then turn on the volume and check your accuracy.

A good intermediate exercise is to make polite, informed guesses about new people you're talking to. Try to determine what they do for a living, what kind of environment they were raised in, whether they were popular in school, and what their birth order is. Then, at some point during the conversation, ask and see if you were correct.

Once you're comfortable doing this, next time you're out with friends, look at a group of two or more people and figure out as much about them as you can. In addition to the details already discussed, try to determine their relationship to one another, if they're local or visiting, and what their general story is.

When you're finished, simply walk over and ask them if you're right. Make sure you smile, ask with genuine curiosity, don't make them uncomfortable, and don't seem like you're making fun of them or judging them. Not only will this give you the feedback you need to improve your calibration, rapport, and cold-reading skills, but it's a great opener—as you'll discover in your field exercise today.

DAY 29

MISSION 1: Step on the Scale

As you learned yesterday, there are three aspects to the game: who you are, what you do, and when and how you do it.

Today we're going to further explore the idea of who you are. It's not easy to make lasting improvements to the characteristics of your personality, but once you begin the process, you'll start moving toward your goals in dating and life as if you were on autopilot. You won't need to whip out the rings routine to demonstrate value, because you'll be demonstrating value simply by existing.

The switches of attraction and desire can be flipped by eight major personality attributes working together. Turn to your Day 29 Briefing, read about them, and rate yourself from 1 to 10 in each category.

If you have been doing the Challenge with a friend, told anyone about your missions, or found a local wing in the Stylelife forums, when you're finished scoring yourself, ask your trusted acquaintance to give you an honest rating in each category as well.

MISSION 2: The Final Sprint

If you haven't yet been on or arranged a date this month, it's time to make it happen.

If you haven't yet received a definite, ironclad confirmation for your dinner party from at least one of the women you've met, it's approach time for you as well.

Tomorrow the Stylelife Challenge ends.

And you have the tools it takes to be a winner. All you have to do is use and implement them.

To make sure no one gets left behind, I've saved one technique for today: the instant conversation starter.

Grab a notebook or a piece of paper. Write at the top, in capital letters, "TOP TEN FILMS." Now number it from one to ten.

Your mission today is to make a list of the top ten films of all time. You're going to play one or two of these in the background, with the sound off, at every party you have. Of course, with such an important task, you're going to need some assistance.

So go to one of the following five locations, where you're most likely to meet friendly, open-minded women:

1. A health-food grocery store such as Trader Joe's or Whole Foods Market
2. The lobby, lounge, bar, or pool area of a major hotel
3. The bookstore, library, cafeteria, or student center of a college
4. A spirituality bookstore, alternative coffeehouse, or yoga studio
5. An event from local newspaper listings that attractive single women are likely to attend, whether it be a wine tasting or a casting call

Make sure that you bring your list and a pen. Fill in five spaces anywhere on the list with film titles. But make sure you leave the number one and number two spaces blank for her valuable input.

Here's a sample script you may want to use: "Hey, you look like you may know something about movies. I'm trying to figure out the top ten films of all time for this weekly movie party I'm starting, and I'm experiencing total brain freeze. Here's what I have so far."

Then show her the list and have her help you fill it out. To disqualify, tease her for choosing frivolous or obvious movies; to create rapport, bond on favorite films. When the energy begins to flag, start a new thread by using an opinion opener, the rings routine, a story from your files, or anything else you've learned this month.

Your goal, of course, is to seed your party, invite her to it, and exchange phone numbers. Since this is the penultimate day of the Challenge, spend as long as it takes until you have a solid number exchange.

This is the first day of the rest of your dating life.

DAY 29 BRIEFING
WHO YOU ARE: THE L.A.S. V.E.G.A.S. SYSTEM

Rate yourself in each of the qualities below on a scale of 1 to 10, where 1 is completely deficient in the trait, 5 is average, and 10 is perfect. Judge yourself not as you see yourself but as you believe others see you. Try to be as honest and realistic as possible. Write your answers in the spaces below.

Looks

At the beginning of the Challenge, you learned that looks have less to do with your physical features than with how you present yourself. Rate yourself on your grooming, posture, eye contact, whether you stand out in a positive way, and if your style attracts the type of women you want to be with.
RATING: _____

SUGGESTION FOR IMPROVEMENT: Study and execute more Day 5 tasks; find role models whose style you admire; make dates to shop for clothing, shoes, and grooming supplies with women you meet.

Adaptability

Ever notice that uptight men tend not to do well with women? This is because they aren't adaptable. Rate yourself on your adventurousness, spontaneity, independence, risk taking, social intelligence, flexibility, and ability to handle new situations and environments.
RATING: _____

SUGGESTION FOR IMPROVEMENT: Write down a few things you'd like to do in your lifetime. Focus not on career or relationship goals but on recreational skills and adventures—learning to scuba dive, taking a safari, building a kit car, or competing in a triathlon. Then circle one of these items and commit to doing it in the next six months. Enter it into your calendar six months from now to make a firm deadline for yourself.

Strength

Strength is the ability to protect a woman and make her feel safe. Some men display this through money or muscle, but those aren't necessary—and often aren't enough. So rate yourself on being an effective communicator, having a powerful frame, living in your own reality, your ability to take care of others, and criteria such as assertiveness, leadership ability, courage, loyalty, decisiveness, and self-assurance.

RATING: _____

SUGGESTION FOR IMPROVEMENT: From the list above, select one attribute you need to work on in order to add a point to your strength. Then start demonstrating it in social situations, whether it's showing you're decisive by ordering for a table of friends at a restaurant or demonstrating your communication ability by talking your way into a store when it's about to close.

Value

As you learned on Day 14, value is one of the key criteria people look for when deciding whom to align with. Value actually consists of three elements: what you think your value is, what she thinks it is, and what impartial observers think it is. Rate yourself on the degree to which you're the leader of a social circle, admired by others, able to teach people things, and comfortable displaying high-status behaviors. Other criteria include being intelligent, interesting, talented, entertaining, successful, self-sufficient, and creative.

RATING: _____

SUGGESTION FOR IMPROVEMENT: Make a list of five reasons a woman would want to see you again after meeting you for fifteen minutes. The list should be based on the value you either project or provide to her. Commit to learning one new skill, game, or attribute to add to that list.

Emotional Connection

This is the home of rapport and abstract concepts like chemistry. It's about possessing qualities that make people feel excited, connected, comfortable, and understood around you, as if they've just met a best friend or soulmate. Rate yourself on your success in finding commonalities with strangers, creating deep rapport with people, being in touch with your feelings, listening closely to others; and on criteria such as compassion, positivity, selflessness, and empathy.

RATING: _____

SUGGESTION FOR IMPROVEMENT: Fear, insecurity, and lack of self-awareness block the ability to emotionally connect with others. Try to spend part of each day communicating, sensing, and existing with an open heart and through your deepest feelings—whatever that means to you. Drop any pretensions, masks, and walls that separate you from others. If you disagree with people, rather than trying to make your point, empathize with what they're feeling. If you're not the type to meditate, then step outside your comfort zone, go to a class or retreat, and try it.

Goals

As discussed on Day 1, goals are defined not by what you do but by your ambitions and what you're capable of doing. Rate yourself on the clarity of your goals, dreams, and hunger for life. You can measure your potential to achieve them by determining if you possess traits like stability, efficiency, perseverance, and the ability to learn quickly.

RATING: _____

SUGGESTION FOR IMPROVEMENT: Review the goals you set for yourself on Day 2. On a separate sheet of paper, write an actual timeline for achieving each goal, with definite benchmarks. Make sure you include any financial requirements or potential complications in your calculations. Adjust this schedule every year based on new insights, information, and accomplishments—and live by it.

Authenticity

An authentic person is happy with himself and embraces even his imperfections. Rate yourself on your congruence—the alignment between the face you show to the world and what you're really like on the inside. Keep in mind that having contradictory sides to your personality doesn't make you incongruent. Having a duality, contradiction, or complications can make you more rich and compelling as a person. But being phony, insincere, or disingenuous does not.

RATING: _____

SUGGESTION FOR IMPROVEMENT: On a piece of paper, write down the qualities you try to portray to the world. Next to each, add a 1 to 10 rating for how closely that quality matches who you really are deep inside. For any quality you rated under a 7, write down the obstacle that prevents it from being true. For example, if you want others to think of you as confident, but you rated your actual feelings of confidence as a 5, then your obstacle is insecurity. If the trait is financial success, then the obstacle is your lack of wealth. Work to remove that obstacle. Sources of help can include self-improvement books, seminars, therapy, or life changes such as a new job, hobby, or social circle. This will not be a short or easy road, but you won't regret taking it.

Self-Worth

This may be the single most important attribute here, and the wellspring from which most of the others flow. Rate yourself on your sense of confidence and worthiness, as well as your lack of fears and insecurities about yourself. Examine your willingness to take up space as you move through the world, how well you accept compliments, how comfortable you are when other people pay attention to you, and how much you deserve the devotion of a woman of the highest caliber. Do you truly believe that you're entitled to the best the world has to offer?

RATING: _____

SUGGESTION FOR IMPROVEMENT: In the end (and you're only one day away), self-worth is what the Stylelife Challenge has been all about. Don't stop learning and improving after Day 30. Continue to examine yourself rigorously, work on your shortcomings, eliminate sticking points, raise the bar for yourself, and develop relationships with positive-minded people. As you experience more and more success, you will recognize, embrace, and exude more and more self-worth.

> **Total Score (all eight categories)** _____
> **L.A.S. V.E.G.A.S. score (total points divided by 8)** _____

In the months to come, your long-term mission is to boost your L.A.S. V.E.G.A.S. score. It's much less work to attract the best when you truly are the best.

DAY

30

MISSION 1: Party Time

You're too busy to handle a big mission today. After all, you have a dinner party to throw. Refer to your Day 24 briefing if you need any help making the final preparations and arrangements.

If you weren't able to invite any women to the party—or you're not sure whether enough people are going to show up—set aside a few hours earlier in the day to make approaches.

Go to a nearby location such as a mall, café, or other area where women gather. Make as many approaches as possible. As soon as you hit the hook point with a woman or group you like, give yourself a time constraint and invite them to your dinner party. If you go home without having recruited any extra guests, don't cancel your party. It's a great opportunity to strengthen your social circle and leadership skills.

Once party time comes around, don't panic if the guests roll in late. It'll all work out great. Enjoy it. Make sure the woman you're interested in is comfortable, but don't pay too much attention to her at the expense of being a generous and enchanting host. Make sure everyone's glasses are always full.

After dinner, if all is going well with your date, ask her to stay behind and help clean up. If your party is at a restaurant or public location, have a second place in mind to go afterward—an interesting bar, lounge, or event on your calendar. If you both drove there, suggest taking one car. This way, you can have some alone time with her.

Consider having this kind of party every week or every month, so that you can begin building a lifestyle that consistently attracts the kind of women you deserve to be dating.

MISSION 2: Congratulate Yourself

Congratulations. You made it to the final day of the Stylelife Challenge.

If you've performed all the previous assignments and feel you've improved yourself in any way this month, then you are a winner. Some people go through their whole lives in darkness.

If you got a date, be proud of yourself for meeting the Challenge objective. If you'd like to share the experience or get feedback on it, describe the details of your approach and date in the Stylelife winner's circle: www.stylelife.com/challenge.

If you didn't get a date, despite completing every mission, then you get an additional assignment today. Go to www.stylelife.com/challenge and listen to the audio lesson titled "Works in Progress." You may find a solution there to whatever held you back.

MISSION 3: Commit to Greatness

So what are you going to do on Day 31 and all the days after that?

Look at how much you improved in a month. Now just imagine the results you could get if you committed to the game for another month, two months, three.

There's still a lot left to learn: what to do on the date; the fundamentals of attraction; techniques of arousal; crossing the physical divide; handling different environments; turning friends into lovers; being more fun; manufacturing chemistry; applying persuasion; leadership; group dynamics; isolation; kissing; winging; body language speed-reading; inner-circle sexual techniques; and hundreds of great routines and advanced concepts. Everything you've learned so far is only the beginning.

The art of social dynamics is much like working out: If you stop going to the gym, your muscles begin to dissipate and return to their former size. So your penultimate mission is to go to www.stylelife.com/Day31 to receive a game plan for the future.

This may be the end of the road on the Stylelife Challenge, but it's the beginning of a new journey.

I'll see you on that journey.

MISSION 4: Into the Looking Glass

Your final task: Look at yourself in the mirror.

Who do you see?

Even though I spent years undergoing an intensive campaign to improve myself, sometimes I'd look in the mirror and see the guy who was never popular and never had a date in high school looking back at me. Despite appearing and acting completely different, I still sometimes saw the world through his eyes.

Similarly, some Challengers I've met went through radical transformations. They looked cool, had good jobs, dated amazing women, and were fun to be around. But when they looked in the mirror, they saw the person they used to be.

So if you don't love, value, and appreciate the guy looking back at you in the mirror, then it's time to change your lenses. I'm not going to ask you to see your true self in the mirror; few of us have that kind of perspective. But instead of seeing the old you in the looking glass, try seeing the person you're becoming. You're going to like him a lot more.

Remember, perception is reality. And when you see yourself as a guy who's socially awkward, you'll act that way and others will treat you that way—no matter what your external appearance and value may be.

But when you see the fun, positive, confident, graceful, socially savvy person you're becoming in the mirror, and consequently start seeing the world through his eyes, people will respond a lot differently to you—because you've just fought the hardest battle and won. You beat your old programming.

So clean up and take a good look at yourself in the mirror. Reflect back to when you examined yourself in the mirror on Day 4 and think about everything you've learned and accomplished since then.

Be aware of your posture, smile, and energy as you look in the mirror. Recall your most successful approach and the way the woman genuinely enjoyed you. Once you see your best self confidently beaming back at you—the guy who any woman would love to be around—take a mental snapshot of that guy. And carry that photograph in your head wherever you go. Because that guy is you.

Welcome to your new reality.

ACKNOWLEDGMENTS

The Stylelife Challenge is the result of lessons from thousands of approaches, years of camaraderie with the master pickup artists from *The Game*, feedback from students around the world, hundreds of books and research papers, and the contributions of the Stylelife Academy coaching team.

There are two contributors, in particular, who deserve special recognition. You've met them already in your briefings:

Don Diego Garcia is a San Francisco–based Stylelife Senior Coach with a heart of gold. He has written scores of the most highly regarded missions and ebooks in recent memory, positively influenced the lives of thousands of students, and helped proofread this book.

Thomas Scott McKenzie is a Midwest-based Stylelife Senior Coach and ace author. He has written for many journals and magazines, from the profound (*Tin House*) to the profane (*Stuff*). In addition to contributing to the briefings, he also helped edit the original multimedia Stylelife Challenge materials into these narrow pages.

Thanks also to Dessi, Haze, Organizer, Masters, Julia Caulder, Maddash, DJ, and especially Phoenix and Rourke for helping out behind the scenes on the earliest incarnation of the Challenge. Stylelife Coaches Evolve, Tommy D, Gypsy, and Bravo also helped make this book possible. The Challenger known as Exception deserves credit for the Village People opener mentioned on Day 18. And Rourke and Michael Gregus also contributed material.

Special thanks also to the seduction gurus who have influenced my life and this book with their teachings, and camaraderie. They include Mystery, now a star of stage and screen; David DeAngelo, who has branched out into the business world; Ross Jeffries, the father of the movement that spawned this madness; Swinggcat, the wizard behind the curtain; and Juggler, a great writer and, now, a married man.

Then there are two men whose names I cannot mention. They are part of a future book. But I owe the idea for the Stylelife Challenge to them. You'll read about them then. But I'd feel remiss if I didn't give them their due. So thanks to . . . those two guys.

The proofreading team consisted of many of the aforementioned characters, along with Anna G., Ersin Pertan, M the G, Todd Strauss, Dr. M. J., Nicole Renee, Aimee Moss, Kelly Gurwitz, Lauren, Evelyn Ng, and Sarah Dowling. Soa Cho and Kristine Harlan did the fact-checking and research, unearthing psychological and scientific papers supporting everything from the time constraint to the L.A.S. V.E.G.A.S. attributes to approaching with a smile.

My most enthusiastic contrafibularities go to the world-class HarperCollins construction team: Carrie Kania, Michael Morrison, David Roth-Ey, Lisa Gallagher, Rachel Romano, Chase Bodine, Cassie Jones, Brittany Hamblin, and Cal Morgan, the fastest editor in the East. Thanks also to Judith Regan, who originally suggested turning the Challenge into a book.

Finally, I'd like to thank you for completing the Challenge and taking control of your reality. The only thing better than hearing the success stories is seeing the before and after photos. You guys are putting *Body for Life* to shame. Respect.

NEIL STRAUSS is the author of the *New York Times* bestseller *The Game*. He is also the coauthor of three *New York Times* bestsellers—Jenna Jameson's *How to Make Love Like a Porn Star*, Mötley Crüe's *The Dirt*, and Marilyn Manson's *The Long Hard Road Out of Hell*—as well as Dave Navarro's *Don't Try This at Home*, a *Los Angeles Times* bestseller. A writer for *Rolling Stone*, Strauss lives in Los Angeles and can be found at www.neilstrauss.com.